The New York Coffee Guide.

2017

Edited by
Jeffrey Young

Author: Allegra Strategies
Reviewers: Richard Ehrlich, Jeremy Hersh, Marisa Kanter & Emma Meltzer
Researchers: Becky Hindley & Laura Newby
Photography: Jael Marschner
& provided by venues
Design: John Osborne
Website: Tim Spring
Publisher: Allegra Publications Ltd

Allegra
PUBLICATIONS

Visit our website:
www.newyorkcoffeeguide.com

🐦 **@NYCoffeeGuide**

f **NYCoffeeGuide**

 newyorkcoffeeguide

All information was accurate at time of going to press.

Published by **Allegra** PUBLICATIONS Ltd © 2017

Walkden House, 10 Melton Street, London, NW1 2EB, UK

Foreword

by **Howard Schultz**, Chairman and CEO, Starbucks Coffee Company

I have always celebrated my New York City origins.

I was born in Brooklyn, in the housing projects of Canarsie. As a kid I played ball on concrete playgrounds, cheered for the Yankees and at 16 worked at a factory in Manhattan's garment district.

The New York City I grew up in was not sophisticated – and neither was its coffee. Then, coffee was freeze-dried, dispensed from vending machines, or a tasteless staple at all-night diners. It was a drink consumed more for its caffeine than savored for its flavors. Habit, not ritual.

Ever since I left the city to attend college, I have returned often. Perhaps my most memorable visit was in 1994, when Starbucks first opened in New York City at 87th Street and Broadway on the Upper West Side. The morning the store opened, a line of curious customers snaked around the block; not many people then had tasted espresso drinks. Coffee as craft was just emerging in America.

More than 20 years later, I still marvel at how this city, coffee, and coffee culture continue to transform. Where West Coast cities once led coffee innovation, the New York City of today has established its own artisanal voice. Aging techniques, flavor infusions, cold coffee combinations and handcrafting have turned neighborhoods throughout the five boroughs into vibrant coffee destinations.

On these streets, New Yorkers and visitors enjoy an eclectic yet accessible variety of coffee experiences. Taste profiles range from simple to complex, and beans are sourced from all over the world, many roasted locally, some right before your eyes.

Most exciting, New Yorkers are more engaged than ever in the beverage's story from farm to cup. They know the origin of their favorite coffees and they know the names of their favorite baristas – in part because the baristas of today are expert, artist, host and friend. Whether working for an independent proprietor or a large purveyor, the men and women who bring coffee to life for their customers are the soul of the city they serve.

For me, New York City will always be a place that honors its past while embracing the present. Coffee's story is no different – a beverage rich with history and always ripe for innovation. I am so proud to be part of coffee's journey, especially as it continues to unfold in what truly is one of the greatest cities in the world.

Contents

Introduction

Welcome to The New York Coffee Guide 2017 – the definitive guide to New York's best craft coffee venues.

The New York Coffee Guide was born in 2012 out of a quest to discover the best coffee venues in New York. This great city has a long, rich coffee house tradition and is now home to a thriving craft coffee scene. With the explosion of coffee venues since our last edition, this year's guide contains an abundance of fantastic coffee locations. The 2017 edition profiles 160 of the best venues.

The New York Coffee Guide has been written to lead coffee lovers around the city on the hunt for a great coffee experience. The main attraction might be the coffee itself or, perhaps, the

excitement of visiting a new and unique coffee shop. Overall, our aim is to encourage fellow coffee lovers to try something different and discover places they otherwise may never have known existed.

In this edition we have expanded the venue content, updated the style of the guide, and added interesting articles written by industry experts. We would like to thank all who have contributed.

Allegra Strategies is an established leader in research and business intelligence for the coffee industry. We have drawn on this research as well as a variety of other sources to compile The New York Coffee Guide. We hope you enjoy it.

Gasoline Alley

About the Guide

Ratings

Every venue featured in The New York Coffee Guide 2017 has been visited and rated by our expert team. The ratings fall into two distinct categories: Coffee Rating and Overall Rating on a score of 1-5, with 5 being the highest possible score. Customer feedback received via The New York Coffee Guide website and app also informs the venue shortlist and the final scores.

Coffee Rating

The Coffee Rating is about much more than just taste in the cup. An excellent coffee experience depends on a host of factors including: barista skills, coffee supplier, equipment, consistency, working processes and coffee presentation. The venue's coffee philosophy and commitment to excellence are also taken into consideration.

Overall Rating

In combination with the Coffee Rating, the Overall Rating reflects the total coffee shop experience for the customer. Factors taken into account include: service, café ambience, venue scale and impact, design and food quality. Feedback from the industry is also taken into consideration.

Key to symbols

Roaster		Disabled access	
Alternative brew methods available		Credit cards accepted	
Decaffeinated coffee available		Wifi available	
Coffee beans sold on site		Alcohol served	
Gluten-free products available		Coffee courses available	
Venue has a loyalty card		Outdoor seating	
Milk alternatives available		Brunch available at weekends	
Restrooms		Cold brew available	
Parent & baby friendly		Computer friendly	

A Brief History of New York Coffee Shops

THE EARLY YEARS

800 AD The coffee plant (Coffea) attracts human interest and consumption as early as 800 AD in the Kaffe region of Ethiopia. According to legend, it was an Ethiopian goat herder named Kaldi who first discovered how animated his herd of goats became after chewing on the red berries.

13TH – 16TH CENTURIES

Coffee berries are brought to the Arabian Peninsula and the first known cultivation of coffee is established in the area known today as Yemen. A crude version of coffee - roasted beans crushed and boiled in water - is developed and by 1475 coffee houses are established in Constantinople, Cairo and throughout Persia.

17TH AND 18TH CENTURIES

Travelers to the Arabian Peninsula bring coffee to Europe and Britain. Coffee houses are established as centers for the exchange of ideas and information, as well as forums for debate.

1650 The first English coffee house is established in Oxford by a Jewish gentleman named Jacob at the Angel in the parish of St Peter.

1668 Coffee is brought to New Amsterdam (Old New York) by Dutch settlers.

1696 Built in the style of the coffee houses of Europe, The King's Arms is the first coffee house established in New York.

1732 The Exchange Coffee House is opened on Broadway and establishes itself as a center for commerce.

1750 The Exchange Coffee House loses favor and is replaced by The Merchants Coffee House (on what is now known as Wall Street), which grows to be the foremost gathering place in the city for trade and political debate.

1765 A warning to the citizens of New York to end their rioting against the Stamp Act is read at The Merchants Coffee House.

1773 The Boston Tea Party, a revolt against the high taxation levied by King George III on tea imported to the New World, sees coffee replace tea as the drink of choice in the colonies.

1784 The Bank of New York, the oldest bank in the country, is founded at The Merchants Coffee House.

1792 The New York Stock Exchange is established at the Tontine Coffee House on Wall Street, where the first public stocks are sold.

19TH AND 20TH CENTURIES

With the rise of industrialization and technological advances, coffee drinking becomes accessible to everyone, not just the elite. People begin drinking it more in their homes and the demand for the beans rises, leading to rapid growth in coffee production.

1840 The Gillies Coffee Company is founded in New York, a company that survives as the oldest coffee merchant in the city.

1850 Folgers Coffee is founded in San Francisco.

1864 The first commercial coffee roasting machine, New York's Jabez Burns' #1 Coffee Roaster, receives a US patent.

1882 The Coffee Exchange of New York begins regulating the coffee trade, setting standards for the traffic of the commodity as well as the quality of the product.

1892 Maxwell House Coffee is founded.

1907 Porto Rico Importing Company opens on Bleecker Street.

1911 The National Coffee Association of the USA is established, the first trade association for the US coffee industry.

1920s As Prohibition takes effect, national coffee sales flourish.

1923 Green Coffee Association of New York founded.

1927 Caffe Reggio opens in Greenwich Village with the first espresso machine in New York.

1946 Coffee consumption in the US hits an all-time high, reaching 19.8 pounds per person per annum, twice what it was in 1900.

1950s / 1960s After WWII, the importation of coffee is impeded. The Pan American Coffee Bureau is established to promote the drinking of coffee and assist its production in Central America. One such promotion is the popularization of the "coffee break".

Italian-style cafés serving espresso and pastries begin to pop up in Greenwich Village and Little Italy. These coffee shops become creative and intellectual centers for artists, writers, musicians, and intellectuals.

1953 Howard Schultz is born in Brooklyn.

1971 Starbucks opens its first store at Pike Place Market in Seattle, Washington.

1982 The Specialty Coffee Association of America (SCAA) is founded.

Late 1980s

After an inspiring visit to Italy, Howard Schultz buys Starbucks and revamps the brand.

1994 Manhattan's first Starbucks store opens on the Upper West Side at 86th Street and Broadway.

1995 Intelligentsia Coffee & Tea opens in Chicago and grows to become one of the major names in the American coffee industry.

1999 Stumptown Coffee Roasters opens in Portland, Oregon.

The Cup of Excellence is established.

LAST DECADE

The 2000s see specialty coffee and the third-wave coffee movement emerge in the US, starting in Portland and Seattle and spreading to California, New York and beyond. This movement focuses on ethical trading, coffee freshness and new roasting techniques.

2000 The first World Barista Championship takes place in Monte Carlo.

2001 Ninth Street Espresso opens in Alphabet City.

2003 Gorilla Coffee opens in Park Slope, Brooklyn.

The first Joe location opened

2005 Café Grumpy established.

2007 La Colombe Torrefaction opens its first New York outpost in Tribeca.

2009 Stumptown Coffee opens its first New York location at The Ace Hotel in Brooklyn.

2010 The Blue Bottle Coffee Company opens its roastery in a converted warehouse in Williamsburg, Brooklyn.

American Michael Phillips wins the World Barista Championship.

2012 The US Barista champion is Katie Carguilo

Australian-owned Toby's Estate opens in Williamsburg, Brooklyn.

The New York Coffee Guide first published.

2013 The US Barista Champion is Pete Licata.

Key openings in the New York coffee scene include Devoción, Rex and Stumptown on West 8th Street.

2014 The US Barista Champion is Laila Ghambari.

Starbucks opens it first reserve store in Williamsburg. Bluestone Lane on Greenwich Avenue and Fika Tower & Bakery are other notable openings.

2015 New York Coffee Festival launched.

The US Barista Champion is Charles Babinski.

Bluestone Lane on East 90th Street open their first store inside a church.

2016 The US Barista Champion is Lemuel Butler.

Taylor St. Baristas open their first New York store after their huge success in London.

New York Coffee Festival returns for a second year.

New York Coffee Guide publishes its second edition.

COFFEE VENUES KEY

◊ TOP 35

Gimme! Coffee

Lower Manhattan

Lower Manhattan is a diverse and exciting area with a variety of identities. The business-savvy Financial District has the hustle and bustle of Wall Street at its heart, while trendy Tribeca is a hip, fashionable neighborhood that overlooks the Hudson River. By night, the Meatpacking District is immensely fashionable, with great shopping, chic restaurants and popular bars and clubs. Most importantly it is home to The World Trade Center.

Black Fox Coffee Co.

70 Pine Street, Manhattan, NY 10005 | **Financial District**

Photo courtesy of the venue

Black Fox is a beautiful new downtown venue, located just around the corner from the South Street Seaport. The space is large and open, designed purposely to emphasize service and make everyone feel at one with the space. Manager Kris Wood makes it clear that he does not want to dictate taste, instead offering a small selection of high quality roasters to provide an element of choice. The fare is Australian inspired, with fresh ingredients prepared by a chef straight from Melbourne. Be sure to try the Australian take on the PB&J, you won't regret it.

www.blackfoxcoffee.com
Subway 2, 3 (Wall St)

MON-FRI. 7:00am – 5:00pm
SAT-SUN. Closed

First opened 2016
Roaster Heart Coffee, Small Batch, Ruby, 49th Parallel, Parlor Coffee
Machine Kees Van Der Westen Spirit, 3 groups
Grinder Nuova Simonelli Mythos Clima Pro x2, Mahlkönig EK 43

Espresso	$3.50
Cappuccino	$4.50
Latte	$5.00

MAP REF. 1

COFFEE 4.50 / 5

OVERALL 4.50 / 5 ★★★★☆

Gotan

130 Franklin Street, Manhattan, NY 10013 | **Tribeca**

A spacious café full of blonde wood and huge windows letting in light, Gotan is a favorite among the well-dressed denizens of Tribeca, and those who work in the area (If you need a primer on Tribeca, three words: Beyoncé lives here). The uniformed and bow-tied baristas are serious about their coffee, made on the fairly unique and handsome ModBar espresso machine, built right into the bar. Go for an expertly made latte.

(212) 431-5200
www.gotannyc.com
Subway 1, 2 (Franklin St)

Sister locations Midtown

MON–FRI.	7:00am – 5:00pm
SAT–SUN.	9:00am – 5:00pm

First opened 2014
Roaster Counter Culture Coffee
Machine ModBar
Grinder Mazzer Luigi

Espresso	$3.50
Cappuccino	$4.25
Latte	$4.75

MAP REF. 2

COFFEE 4.25 / 5	🫘🫘🫘🫘🫘	OVERALL 4.25 / 5	★★★★★

Irving Farm Coffee Roasters
Lower Manhattan Fulton Center, Manhattan, NY 10038 | **Financial District**

While most of Irving's early venues are very much 'Old New York', the newest is all about new, new, new. Plunked down in the heart of the Fulton Center transit hub, it is inevitably a place where commuters abound. But it's also a good place to sit and watch the world go by, and to marvel at the shifting patterns of light cast down by the "sky-reflector net" in the building's skylight. Irving's coffee is outstanding, whether pour-over or espresso-based, and the latte art is a thing of true beauty.

(646) 918-7761
www.irvingfarm.com
Subway 4, 5, A, C, J, Z (Fulton St)

Sister locations Gramercy / Grand Central Terminal / Lower East Side / Upper East Side / Upper West Side

MON–FRI.	7:00am – 7:00pm
SAT–SUN.	8:00am – 6:00pm

First opened 2016
Roaster Irving Farm Coffee Roasters
Machine La Marzocco Linea PB, 3 groups
Grinder Nuova Simonelli Mythos Clima Pro

Espresso	$3.25
Cappuccino	$4.25
Latte	$4.75

MAP REF. **3**

COFFEE 4.50 / 5 🫘 🫘 🫘 🫘 🫘

OVERALL 4.25 / 5 ★ ★ ★ ★ ⯨

Kaffe 1668

401 Greenwich Street, Manhattan, NY 10013 | **Tribeca**

After a leisurely walk in Hudson River Park, there are few better places to relax and refuel than Kaffe 1668 - as long as you can find a seat. At lunchtime especially, this place is crazy-busy. The big, low-lit room is a pleasure to be in, with zany décor dominated by dozens of cute little fluffy sheep. But it isn't the sheep that get people flocking here. The coffee is made to exacting standards even when crowds are huge, and sandwiches, salads and fresh-squeezed juices provide non-caffeinated sustenance of superior quality.

(646) 559-2637
www.kaffe1668.com
Subway A, C, E (Canal St)

Sister locations Lower Manhattan / Midtown

MON-FRI.	6:30am - 8:00pm
SAT-SUN.	7:00am - 7:00pm

First opened 2012
Roaster Landskap
Machine Synesso, 3 groups
Grinder Mahlkönig EK 43, Mazzer Luigi Robur E

Espresso	$3.25
Cappuccino	$4.50
Latte	$4.75

MAP REF. 4

COFFEE 4.25 / 5

OVERALL 4.25 / 5 ★★★★☆

8

La Colombe

67 Wall Street, Manhattan, NY 10005 | **Financial District**

Photo: La Colombe

La Colombe's Wall Street location is a small place that does a lot of takeout business, which increases your chance of finding a free table. And it's a temptation that's easy to give in to; this attractive place, dominated by pale wood, provides a quiet haven on the Financial District's main drag. Latte art is exceptional, as at their other locations, and they serve both cold brew and latte "on tap." A combination of the two, called Black and Tan, is a wonderfully zingy and invigorating drink.

(212) 220-0415
www.lacolombe.com
Subway 2, 3 (Wall St)

Sister locations Chelsea / Hudson Square / Noho / Soho / Tribeca

| **MON–FRI.** | 6:00am – 6:30pm |
| **SAT–SUN.** | 7:00am – 6.30pm |

First opened 2015
Roaster La Colombe Coffee Roasters
Machine La Marzocco GB5, 3 groups
Grinder Nuova Simonelli Mythos

Espresso	$2.50
Cappuccino	$4.00
Latte	$4.00

MAP REF. 5

| COFFEE 4.50 / 5 | 🌰🌰🌰🌰🌰🌰 | OVERALL 4.25 / 5 | ★★★★⭑ |

Laughing Man

184 Duane Street, Manhattan, NY 10014 | **Tribeca**

Photo: Compassandtwire

This tiny Tribeca café serves up an excellent cup of coffee for a great cause. Inspired by a trip to Ethiopia, Hugh Jackman opened The Laughing Man café in order to provide a market for coffee farmers in developing countries. The café is quite crowded during peak hours, but it serves only as a testament to the quality of their roasts, and the wait is always worth it. The best part - one hundred percent of Hugh Jackman's proceeds are donated to the Laughing Man Foundation, supporting social entrepreneurs around the world.

(212) 680-1111
www.laughingmanfoundation.org/cafe
Subway 1, 2, 3 (Chambers St)

MON-FRI. 6:30am - 7:00pm
SAT-SUN. 7:00am - 7:00pm

First opened 2009
Roaster Laughing Man Coffee
Machine Faema E61, 2 groups
Grinder Nuova Simonelli Mythos

Espresso $2.75
Cappuccino $3.65
Latte $4.10

MAP REF. **6**

| COFFEE 4.25 / 5 | 🫘🫘🫘🫘🫘 | OVERALL 4.25 / 5 | ★★★★⯪ |

10

R & R Coffee

76 Fulton Street, Manhattan, NY 10038 | **Financial District**

Wall Street is on its doorstep, but in spirit and atmosphere R&R is more akin to the Fulton Street Market, also just a step away. Far from being a slick, money-talks kind of Financial District operation, this is a laid-back neighborhood place - more Main Street than Wall Street. Coffee comes from a changing selection of roasters, such as Brooklyn Roasting Company and Parlor Coffee Roasters. It's crafted with care and includes stunning latte art. There's also an extensive list of cold drinks. Bought-in baked goods are rich enough to make love handles at first sight.

(646) 449-8908
Subway 2, 3 (Fulton St)

MON-FRI.	7:00am - 7:00pm
SAT-SUN.	8:00am - 7:00pm

First opened 2013
Roaster Multiple roasters
Machine La Marzocco, 3 groups
Grinder Mahlkönig EK 43, Mazzer Luigi Super Jolly

Espresso	$2.75
Cappuccino	$3.90
Latte	$3.90

MAP REF. **7**

COFFEE 4.25 / 5   OVERALL 4.00 / 5 ★★★★☆

Two Hands Tribeca

251 Church Street, Manhattan, NY 10013 | **Tribeca**

Two Hands deserves a loud clap for looks, variety, and vibe. This big Tribeca room looks great and hums with activity from a crowd that seems mostly locals rather than workers. The owners are Australian, and the menu does the whole Oz thing - make it healthy, but make it look and taste great - very well. Grab a table if you're eating. But if you just crave a well-made coffee and some quality time with your smartphone, settle in at the bar in the back of the room.

www.twohandsnyc.com
Subway A, C, E (Canal St)

Sister locations Soho

MON-SUN.	8:00am - 12:00am

First opened 2016
Roaster Café Integral
Machine La Marzocco Strada, 2 groups
Grinder Compak F8

Espresso	$3.00
Cappuccino	$4.00
Latte	$4.50

MAP REF. **8**

COFFEE 4.25 / 5   OVERALL 4.25 / 5 ★★★★☆

Voyager Espresso

110 William Street, Manhattan, NY 10038 | **Financial District**

Ignore the address: the easiest way to find Voyager is through the John Street subway entrance. However you get here, it's well worth the voyage. This unlikely location houses one of the most distinctively elegant-looking coffee spots in town - the silver-painted chipboard is particularly unique. More importantly, it houses seriously terrific espresso drinks. They use beans from an assortment of roasters, including Portland stars Heart and Roseline, and get fabulous results through expert handling. If you love coffee (and talking about coffee with friendly baristas), Voyager is a genius subterranean heaven.

(646) 885-6792
www.voyagerespresso.com
Subway 2, 3 (Fulton St)

MON-FRI.	7:30am – 5:00pm
SAT-SUN.	Closed

First opened 2015
Roaster Multiple roasters
Machine Synesso Hydra, 3 groups
Grinder Mahlkönig K30, Mahlkönig EK 43

Espresso	$3.50
Cappuccino	$4.25
Latte	$4.25 / $4.75

MAP REF. **9**

COFFEE 4.50 / 5

OVERALL 4.50 / 5 ★★★★½

ROCKET ESPRESSO AT HOME

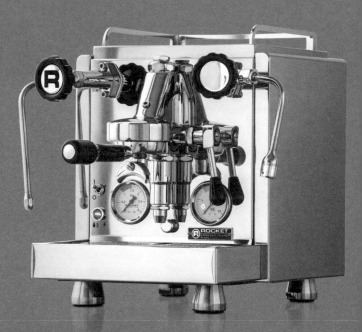

East Village & Lower East Side

The East Village and surrounding areas all have a laidback, colourful vibe. Tompkins Square Park in Alphabet City and the range of vibrant off-Broadway theatres in the East Village are worth a visit, while the Lower East Side is packed with trendy shops, vintage stores, contemporary art galleries, rich local history and vibrant nightlife. The neighborhood still retains much of its Jewish heritage in the buildings, restaurants and synagogues that were established by immigrant communities during the 20th century.

Abraço

81 East 7th Street, Manhattan, NY 10003 | **East Village**

No one does tiny like Abraço does tiny. Get more than six people in there and the place feels packed. But there's a counter-height table outside if you feel like joining the lively local community. It revolves around this outstanding source of beautifully crafted drinks from the company's own roaster. Most people come for coffee to go. If you can grab one of the few seats, you'll feel the social buzz as well as the caffeinated variety. Abraço means hug in Portuguese; an appropriate name.

www.abraconyc.com
Subway 4, 6 (Astor Pl)

MON.	Closed
TUE-SAT.	8:00am - 6:00pm
SUN.	9:00am - 6:00pm

First opened 2007
Roaster Abraço
Machine La Marzocco Linea, 2 groups
Grinder Mazzer Luigi

Espresso	$2.00
Cappuccino	$3.50
Latte	$3.50

MAP REF. **10**

COFFEE 4.50 / 5 | **OVERALL** 4.00 / 5 ★★★★☆

Box Kite East Village

TOP 35

115 St Marks Place, Manhattan, NY 10003 | **East Village**

Box Kite is unusual in having an ever-changing pool of guest roasters, which leads to great variety in what's on offer. Their brewed coffees change every single day and their standards are consistently high. And even though the place is tiny (just three tables and a counter seating eight people), it aims for big things with its innovative coffee cocktails, ambitious cooking, and evening tasting menus by talented guest chefs. From its beautifully made brews to its sensational cooking, Box Kite is an all-round high flyer.

(212) 574-8201
www.boxkitenyc.com
Subway N, R (8th St - NYU) or 6 (Astor Pl)

Sister locations Upper West Side

MON.-SUN. 7:00am - 7:00pm

First opened 2014
Roaster Rotating roasters
Machine Synesso Hydra, 2 groups
Grinder Mazzer Luigi Robur, Mahlkönig EK 43

Espresso	$3.50
Cappuccino	$4.50
Latte	$4.75

MAP REF. **11**

COFFEE 4.50 / 5 | **OVERALL** 4.25 / 5 ★★★★☆

Café Grumpy Lower East Side

13 Essex Street, Manhattan, NY 10002 | **Lower East Side**

We're not sure how many visits it takes before you get greeted by name in this tiny place, but we do know that most customers seem to have met the minimum. The very un-grumpy welcome is at its warmest here, from the big smile to always-remembered regular orders to advice about which baked goods to order. ('Do you want healthy or sweet?') All this comes with expertly pulled shots, great latte art and fabulous brewed coffees. 'We want to add to the community,' says the staff here. And they certainly do.

(212) 477-7582
www.cafegrumpy.com
Subway F (East Broadway)

Sister locations Chelsea / Grand Central Terminal / Greenpoint / Midtown / Park Slope

MON-FRI.	7:00am - 7:00pm
SAT-SUN.	7:30am - 7:00pm

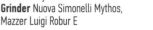

First opened 2011
Roaster Café Grumpy Coffee
Machine Synesso
Grinder Nuova Simonelli Mythos, Mazzer Luigi Robur E

Espresso	$3.00
Cappuccino	$4.00
Latte	$4.50

MAP REF. **12**

COFFEE 4.50 / 5	OVERALL 4.25 / 5

Café Henrie

116 Forsyth Street, Manhattan, NY 10002 | **Chinatown**

Café Henrie may have a French name, but it pays homage to a concept of hipness that's 100 percent downtown Manhattan. Owner Andre Saraiva is an artist, and the visuals here are full of treats and surprises, from the artwork hung on a pegboard, to the one-of-a-kind espresso cups. The young clientele pile in for beautifully made coffee and for fashionably healthy 'Dragon Bowl' salads. Venues that set out to be hip are sometimes too much like someone else's formula. The only formula here is Henrie's own, and it's executed with flair - and a smile.

www.cafehenrie.com
Subway J, Z (Bowery), B, D (Grand St)

MON-TUE.	8:30am - 6:00pm
WED-SUN.	8:30am - 10:30pm

First opened 2015
Roaster Counter Culture Coffee
Machine La Marzocco Linea, 2 groups
Grinder Nuova Simonelli Mythos

Espresso	$3.00
Cappuccino	$4.00
Latte	$4.00

MAP REF. **13**

COFFEE 4.00 / 5	OVERALL 4.00 / 5

Caffe Vita Lower East Side

124 Ludlow Street, Manhattan, NY 10002 | **Lower East Side**

Caffe Vita's Lower East Side operation is a tiny but trendy hole in the wall, with seating for three people. If you're lucky enough to sit, you'll enjoy watching an exemplary operation at work. The baristas make cup after cup for thirsty locals, many of them regulars, while talking, filling growlers and tending lovingly to the gleaming Kees machine. Vita has its origins on the West Coast, and the pedigree shows in the effortless combination of hip, friendly, casual, and ultra-professional. Make sure to check out the artisan roaster at the back of the room.

(212) 260-VITA
www.caffevita.com
Subway F (Delancy St)

MON-FRI.	7:00am - 9:00pm
SAT-SUN.	8:00am - 9:00pm

First opened 2012
Roaster Caffe Vita
Machine Kees van der Westen, 3 groups
Grinder Mazzer Luigi Robur E

Espresso	$3.25
Cappuccino	$4.65
Latte	$4.65

Sister locations Bushwick

MAP REF. **14**

COFFEE 4.25 / 5

OVERALL 4.00 / 5 ★★★★☆

City of Saints East Village

79 East 10th Street, Manhattan, NY 10003 | **East Village**

East Village & Lower East Side

With its extremely friendly service and thoughtful but effortless design (lots of wood and epiphytes), City of Saints is remarkably welcoming and relaxed for the often sharp-edged, fast-paced East Village neighborhood. Go for a single-origin cold brew - they roast their own beans in Bushwick - and skip the milk to fully taste its light, floral, black-tea-esque complexity. If you're in the mood for something sweet, try the lavender agave latte (available hot or iced), which has a nice rosemary flavour peeking out behind the agave.

(646) 590-1624
www.cityofsaintscoffee.com
Subway 6 (Astor Place), N, Q, R (8th St - NYU)

MON-FRI.	7:00am - 7:00pm
SAT.	8:00am - 6:00pm
SUN.	9:00am - 5:00pm

First opened 2014
Roaster City of Saints Coffee Roasters
Machine ModBar
Grinder Mazzer Luigi Robur E

Espresso	$3.00
Cappuccino	$3.75
Latte	$4.25

Sister locations Bushwick

MAP REF. **15**

COFFEE 4.50 / 5	🫘 🫘 🫘 🫘 🫘	OVERALL 4.50 / 5	★ ★ ★ ★ ⯪

18

El Rey

100 Stanton Street, Manhattan, NY 10018 | **Lower East Side**

TOP
35

This unique shop stands out with superior coffee and a deliciously inventive fare. The kitchen is small but mighty, with food focused on fresh vegetables and unique baked goods. They use locally roasted Parlor Coffee and have cold brew on tap. This compact shop is bright and lively, accented with greenery and warm light which bounces off mirrors adorning the walls. Relax and enjoy this bustling trendy eatery and café.

(212) 260-3950
www.elreynyc.com
Subway F (Delancy St)

MON-FRI.	7:00am - 10:00pm
SAT-SUN.	8:00am - 10:00pm

First opened 2013
Roaster Parlor Coffee
Machine La Marzocco Strada
Grinder Mazzer Luigi Robur

Espresso	$2.50
Cappuccino	$3.75
Latte	$4.25

MAP REF. 16

COFFEE
4.25 / 5

OVERALL
4.50 / 5
★★★★⯪

Everyman Espresso East Village

136 East 13th Street, Manhattan, NY 10003 | **East Village**

Everyman shares its space with the lobby of the Classic Stage Company theatre, but to say that it's the best theatre-lobby coffee you've ever had would not do this place justice. This is a serious coffee shop in its own right; the fact that Meryl Streep might brush past your table on her way into the theatre is merely a pleasant side effect. Everyman baristas are fanatical, expert and approachable, while the Counter Culture espresso is smooth and reliable. Everyman is a must visit.

www.everymanespresso.com
Subway L (3rd Ave)

Sister locations Soho

MON.	7:00am - 7:00pm
TUE-FRI.	7:00am - 8:00pm
SAT.	8:00am - 8:00pm
SUN.	8:00am - 7:00pm

First opened 2007
Roaster Counter Culture Coffee
Machine La Marzocco Linea, 2 groups
Grinder Nuova Simonelli Mythos

Espresso	$3.50
Cappuccino	$4.25
Latte	$5.00

MAP REF. **17**

| COFFEE 4.50 / 5 | 🍩🍩🍩🍩🍩 | OVERALL 4.25 / 5 | ★★★★☆ |

20

Gasoline Alley Coffee Noho

TOP 35

325 Lafayette Street, Manhattan, NY 10012 | **Noho**

Gasoline Alley's Lafayette Street location is the perfect place to pop in and refuel during a long day of shopping. The warehouse aesthetic is made chic - fitting in effortlessly with the Noho vibe. Customers flow in and out of this busy shop, whose stripped down seasonal menu prides quality above all else. Those with a sweet tooth ought to pair their beverage with a delicious chocolate chip cookie. During the summer heat, this shop serves a small selection of refreshing organic iced teas

www.gasolinealleycoffee.com
Subway 6 (Bleecker St) or B, D, F, M (Broadway - Lafayette)

Sister locations Soho

MON-FRI.	7:00am - 7:00pm
SAT-SUN.	8:00am - 7:00pm

First opened 2011
Roaster Intelligentsia Coffee
Machine La Marzocco GB5, 3 groups
Grinder Mazzer Luigi Robur E

Espresso	$2.75
Cappuccino	$4.00
Latte	$4.25

MAP REF. **18**

COFFEE 4.50 / 5

OVERALL 4.50 / 5 ★★★★⯪

21

Hi-Collar

214 East 10th Street, Manhattan, NY 10003 | **East Village**

This wondrous concept shop specializes in variety of both taste and form. At night, this elegantly designed shop transforms into a sake bar but during the day, it focuses on coffee with lots of choice. You're handed a beautifully bound menu when you sit at the sleek 13-seat bar, lit by stained glass lamps above. Flip through and you'll find a special house blend and multiple single origin coffees from Counter Culture. Hi-Collar offers six different manual brewing options, so you can adventure through processes and tastes.

(212) 777-7018
hi-collar.com
Subway 6 (Astor Place) or L (1st Ave)

MON-SUN.   11:00am - 5:00pm
                 (for coffee)

First opened 2013
Roaster Counter Culture Coffee, Madcap, George Howell, Ceremony Coffee Roasters
Grinder Ditting KF804

MAP REF. **19**

COFFEE
4.25 / 5

OVERALL
4.25 / 5   ★★★★⯪

22

La Colombe Torrefaction

400 Lafayette Street, Manhattan, NY 10003 | **Noho**

La Colombe's big Noho location always seems to be packed, day or evening. The lines get particularly enormous in the spacious, and very beautiful corner room during the lunch rush, but ample staffing levels and good systems keep them moving through at a reasonable pace. Grabbing a table is a different matter, not that customers ordering to go will care about that. What draws them in is really fine coffee, with single-origin espresso, drip and pour-over given special prominence. Despite plenty of competition, La Colombe remains a high flyer.

(212) 677-5834
www.lacolombe.com
Subway 6 (Astor Place) or N, R (8th St - NYU)

Sister locations Chelsea / Financial District / Hudson Square / Soho / Tribeca

MON-SUN.   7:30am - 6:30pm

Roaster La Colombe Coffee Roasters
Machine La Marzocco GB5, 4 groups
Grinder Nuova Simonelli Mythos

Espresso	$3.00
Cappuccino	$4.00
Latte	$4.00

MAP REF. 20

COFFEE 4.75 / 5

OVERALL 4.75 / 5 ★★★★★

The Lazy Llama

72 East 1st Street, Manhattan, NY 10002 | **East Village**

This offshoot of Hell's Kitchen's The Jolly Goat has a name that fits its leisurely vibe. In the warm months, the tiny shop's front windows swing open and the whole place feels like it's outdoors. Serving Stumptown roasted espresso and a lovely drip by Sweetleaf, the delicious coffee goes hand in hand with its stripped back decor of reclaimed wood and copper tables.
A handy, user-friendly drawing on the chalk board above the bar explains the difference between a latte, flat white, macchiato, etc. Order a silky, rich cold brew (sometimes single-origin) and watch the East village rush by.

(646) 509-8957
Subway F (Second Ave)

MON-SAT. 7:00am - 7:00pm
SUN. 8:00am - 7:00pm

First opened 2016
Roaster Stumptown Coffee Roasters, Sweetleaf Coffee
Machine La Marzocco
Grinder Mazzer Luigi Major

Espresso $3.25
Cappuccino $4.00
Latte $4.50

MAP REF. **21**

COFFEE 4.25 / 5

OVERALL 4.25 / 5

Ludlow Coffee Supply

176 Ludlow Street, Manhattan, NY 10002 | **Lower East Side**

A wall of glass windows separates Ludlow Coffee Supply from its sister business, Ludlow Barber Supply, which is a full-service barbershop. The management also owns next door's ultra-popular chicken-and-waffles-joint, Sweet Chick. Ludlow roasts its own beans in Red Hook, and the espresso is so strong that their latte (made with Battenkill milk) tastes like some cortados you've had. But the real standout is the bourbon vanilla latte-made with real vanilla and bourbon, and almost no added sugar, which once and for all dispels the notion that a vanilla latte shouldn't be a drink of choice.

(212) 777-7465
www.ludlowcoffeesupply.com
Subway F (Delancy St)

MON-SUN. 8:00am - 8:00pm

First opened 2016
Roaster Ludlow Coffee Supply
Machine La Marzocco GB5, 2 groups
Grinder Mazzer Luigi Kony E

Espresso $3.25
Cappuccino $3.75
Latte $4.00

MAP REF. 22

COFFEE 4.25 / 5

OVERALL 4.25 / 5 ★★★★⯪

25

Ninth Street Espresso East Village

341 East 10th Street, Manhattan, NY 10009 | **East Village**

East Village & Lower East Side

Ninth Street Espresso features regularly in lists of New York's best espresso, and there's good reason for this reputation: The coffee is awesome. Ninth Street has been doing its own roasting since 2013, and total control from green beans to pulled shots yields beautiful results. There are tables at the front of this small location, but sitting at the bar gives you the chance to talk to the friendly - and exceptionally skilled - baristas.

(212) 777-3508
www.ninthstreetespresso.com
Subway L (1st Ave)

Sister locations Alphabet City / Chelsea / Downtown Brooklyn / Midtown East

MON-SUN.   7:00am - 8:00pm

First opened 2008
Roaster Ninth Street Espresso
Machine La Marzocco GB5, 2 groups
Grinder Mazzer Luigi

Espresso $3.00

MAP REF. 23

COFFEE 4.50 / 5	OVERALL 4.25 / 5

Ost Cafe

441 East 12th Street, Manhattan, NY 10009 | **East Village**

Photo: @escapeyourdesk

This Central European inspired café prides itself on being a "home away from home" for its customers, whether you choose to sit-in or take your cappuccino to-go. Espresso is switched up daily, between PT's and Intelligentsia, and single origins are available for flavor-filled cold brew. The space is as versatile as its coffee selection: comfortable workspace by day, romantic atmosphere by night. If you frequent by day, be sure to come back when the lights go down, when poetry readings and jazz performances are hosted.

(212) 477-5600
www.ostcafenyc.com
Subway L (First Ave)

Sister locations Lower East Side

MON-FRI.	7:30am - 10:00pm
SAT-SUN.	8:30am - 10:00pm

First opened 2008
Roaster PT's Coffee Roasting Co, Intelligentsia
Machine La Marzocco, 2 groups
Grinder Mazzer Luigi

Espresso	$2.75
Cappuccino	$4.25
Latte	$4.50

MAP REF. **24**

COFFEE 4.25 / 5

OVERALL 4.25 / 5 ★★★★✭

The Roost

222 Avenue B, Manhattan, NY 10009 | **East Village**

Photo courtesy of the venue

The Roost ticks so many Lower East Side boxes you'd think they had an algorithm for peak hipsterdom. Bare brick, distressed wood, gleaming tiles, craft beers, cool cocktails, Balthazar pastries - it's all here. But if it sounds calculating, it comes across as friendly and sincere. Service is sweet, and rather than pushing customers in the direction of milky espresso-based drinks, they make a big feature of their single-origin Brooklyn Roasting Company coffees brewed or made in the French press. At night the Roost is a bar, and - understandably - it gets crowded.

(646) 918-6700
www.theroostnyc.com
Subway L (1st Ave)

MON-SUN. 7:00am - 2:00am

First opened 2013
Roaster Brooklyn Roasting Co.
Machine La Marzocco Linea, 2 groups
Grinder Mazzer Luigi

Espresso	$2.50
Cappuccino	$4.00
Latte	$4.00

MAP REF. **25**

COFFEE 4.25 / 5

OVERALL 4.25 / 5 ★★★★

Spreadhouse

116 Suffolk Street, Manhattan, NY 10002 | **Lower East Side**

Walk in to Spreadhouse once and you might not want to leave ever again. That's partly because of the look and feel of the place, with oriental carpets a major decorative element in the high-ceilinged ex-industrial space. Customers lounge on the kaftan-lined seats (and sometimes on the floor) as if they were at home. Many treat the place as their office, and friends meet up for more sociable activities. Coffee is well made, with or without milk, by ultra-friendly baristas. During the day, light rolls in through the big windows. At night, the atmosphere becomes moody and seductive, and caffeine gives way to alcohol.

(646) 524-6353
www.spreadhousecoffee.com
Subway J, M (Essex St)

MON-FRI.   7:30am - 12:00am
SAT-SUN.   8:00am - 12:00am

First opened 2015
Roaster Joe
Machine La Marzocco Linea, 2 groups
Grinder Nuova Simonelli Mythos One Clima Pro, Mahlkönig EK43

Espresso $3.00
Cappuccino $4.50
Latte $5.00

MAP REF. 26

COFFEE 4.50 / 5

OVERALL 4.50 / 5   ★★★★⯪

Whynot

175 Orchard Street, Manhattan, NY 10002 | **Lower East Side**

Whynot packs in customers despite the Lower East Side competition, especially those seeking to combine caffeine-time with keyboard-time: you're just as likely to hear click-click as talk-talk in this office-away-from home. Those looking up from their devices get a good view of bare brick and big windows with a high ceiling. The coffee comes from Toby's Estate, and it's well made; big jugs of self-service water complete the picture. A table by the window, or a bench outside, is the best place to perch.

(646) 682-9065
Subway F (2nd Ave)

MON-FRI.	8:30am - 8:30pm
SAT-SUN.	9:30am - 9:00pm

First opened 2013
Roaster Toby's Estate Coffee
Machine La Marzocco, 4 groups
Grinder Mazzer Luigi Robur E

Espresso	$3.27
Cappuccino	$4.36
Latte	$4.36

East Village & Lower East Side

MAP REF. **27**

COFFEE 4.25 / 5

OVERALL 4.25 / 5 ★★★★✩

RE

SMOOTH SCOTCH
WHISKY +
**LUSCIOUS DUTCH
CREAM**

f facebook.com/themagnumcream

@themagnumcream

Variety Coffee

Soho & Neighboring

Soho refers to South of Houston Street and is home to some of New York's best shopping with a variety of stores from trendy boutiques and upscale designers to highstreet favorites and chains. Originally an artist's haven before making way for the shopping district, Soho is a firm favorite for residential loft living. Neighboring Nolita, deriving from North of Little Italy, extends the shopping district and includes some of the best kept secrets.

Café Integral at American Two Shot

135 Grand Street, Manhattan, NY 10013 | **Soho**

Café Integral roasts beans exclusively from Nicaragua, fostering close relationships with the farmers who grow them. Integral opened this outpost inside American Two Shot, a trendy boutique where their bar nestles in among the designer rails. They offer sweet bites like shortbread cookies to go with their delicately brewed coffees. Hang out and browse around to see what's both the fashion and coffee du jour.

(305) 773-3066
www.cafeintegral.com
Subway N, Q, R (Canal St), 4, 6 (Canal St)

| MON–FRI. | 8:30am – 5:00pm |
| SAT–SUN. | 11:00am – 5:00pm |

First opened 2013
Roaster Café Integral
Machine La Marzocco Strada
Grinder Compak F10, Compak PRK80

Espresso $3.00
Cappuccino $3.75
Latte $4.00

MAP REF. **28**

COFFEE 4.00 / 5 — OVERALL 4.00 / 5 ★★★★☆

Café Select

212 Lafayette Street, Manhattan, NY 10012 | **Soho**

You'd be forgiven for thinking that Café Select's name refers to the select few who are able to get a table: from breakfast through the cocktail hour and dinner, this Soho eatery is hugely popular. It looks great at any hour, with its long marble bar, whitewashed brick walls and tiny ceiling lights reminiscent of a starry night. While most people come for a meal, excellent baked goods make a great accompaniment to espresso-based coffees of impeccable quality. If tables are all full, select a bar stool and settle in.

(212) 925-9322
www.cafeselectnyc.com
Subway 4, 6 (Spring St) or N, R (Prince St) or B, D, F, M (Broadway - Lafayette St)

| MON–FRI. | 8:00am – 1:00am |
| SAT–SUN. | 9:00am – 2:00am |

First opened 2009
Roaster Stumptown Coffee Roasters
Machine La Marzocco
Grinder La Marzocco Swift

Espresso $4.00
Cappuccino $5.00
Latte $5.00

MAP REF. **29**

COFFEE 4.00 / 5 — OVERALL 4.00 / 5 ★★★★☆

Everyman Espresso Soho

301 West Broadway, Manhattan, NY 10013 | **Soho**

Everyman enlivens the statutory bare brick walls with colorful tiles reminiscent of a Mondrian painting, and with well-designed lighting they make the room a visual delight. That would be reason enough to come here, but the drinks - proclaimed as "Damn Fine Coffee" in lettering on windows, grinders and elsewhere - make a visit even more urgent. The gleaming Simonelli is used to pull fabulous shots, including single-origin specials. People come with kids, friends, devices and headphones. It's a nice mix, producing a friendly neighborhood café with real charm.

www.everymanespresso.com
Subway A, C, E (Canal St)

Sister locations East Village

MON-FRI.	8:00am - 7:00pm
SAT.	9:00am - 6:00pm
SUN.	9:00am - 5:00pm

First opened 2013
Roaster Counter Culture Coffee
Machine La Marzocco Strada, 3 groups
Grinder Nuova Simonelli Mythos Clima Pro

Espresso	$3.50
Cappuccino	$4.25
Latte	$5.00

MAP REF. **30**

COFFEE 4.50 / 5 🫘🫘🫘🫘🫘

OVERALL 4.25 / 5 ★★★★✬

Gasoline Alley Coffee Nolita

154 Grand Street, Manhattan, NY 10013 | **Nolita**

Soho & Neighboring

At Gasoline Alley's Nolita location, the group-heads on the espresso machine outnumber the seats. Three of one, two of the other. However the irresistible baked goods (dive for a donut if you see one) will certainly sweeten your stay. They need three groups because people pile in for cups to go, everything is made well using Intelligentsia beans. Gasoline Alley provides the fuel for local workers and residents with cheerful efficiency, which they guzzle down eagerly.

www.gasolinealleycoffee.com
Subway 6 (Canal St)

Sister locations Noho

MON–FRI.	7:00am – 7:00pm
SAT–SUN.	8:00am – 7:00pm

First opened 2011
Roaster Intelligentsia Coffee
Machine La Marzocco GB5, 3 groups
Grinder Mazzer Luigi Robur E

Espresso	$2.75
Cappuccino	$4.00
Latte	$4.25

MAP REF. **31**

COFFEE 4.50 / 5

OVERALL 4.25 / 5 ★★★★⯨

Gimme! Coffee Nolita

228 Mott Street, Manhattan, NY 10012 | **Nolita**

This Nolita outpost of the Ithaca-based roastery is an unassuming gem. It's nothing flashy, just the model of a local café where lots of regulars come through, and everyone gets a warm welcome. Most people come in for drinks to go, but those who drink on the premises get the full benefit of exquisite latte art on the well-made latte and cappuccino. Sit on the bench outside if weather permits and watch the world go by.

(212) 226-4011
buy.gimmecoffee.com
Subway F (2nd Ave)

Sister locations Williamsburg

MON-FRI. 7:00am - 7:00pm
SAT-SUN. 8:00am - 7:00pm

First opened 2008
Roaster Gimme! Coffee
Machine La Marzocco Strada, 2 groups
Grinder Mazzer Luigi

Espresso $3.00
Cappuccino $3.75
Latte $4.00

MAP REF. **32**

COFFEE 4.25 / 5

OVERALL 4.25 / 5 ★★★★

Greecologies

379 Broome Street, Manhattan, NY 10013 | **Soho**

Situated in the heart of Soho, Greecologies is a must-visit venue. Authentic Greek Yogurt from grass-fed cows is made on site; you can watch it being produced through the large viewing window in the back. The fare is largely Greek inspired yogurts and salads, and their coffee is equally unique. Choose from typical espresso-based beverages, a variety of matcha, or try their grass-fed butter coffee. On a lovely day, take advantage of their private outdoor seating, with greenery and a sense of serenity that will truly make you forget that you're in the middle of Manhattan.

www.greecologies.com
Subway J, Z (Bowery)

| MON-FRI. | 8:00am - 8:00pm |
| SAT-SUN. | 9:00am - 8:00pm |

First opened 2014
Roaster Intelligentsia Coffee
Machine La Marzocco, 2 groups
Grinder Mazzer Luigi

Espresso	$3.25
Cappuccino	$4.00 / $4.50
Latte	$4.00 / $4.50

MAP REF. 33

Soho & Neighboring

COFFEE 4.25 / 5 OVERALL 4.50 / 5 ★★★★½

Ground Support Cafe

399 West Broadway, Manhattan, NY 10012 | **Soho**

Shoppers and local creatives comprise a constant stream of devotees to this oasis of great coffee in bustling Soho. If you can't get a seat at one of the rustic picnic tables, don't worry, the bench outside is even more pleasant. You can't go wrong with an espresso drink, but the delicate, nuanced pour-over here is truly a must.

(212) 219-8722
www.groundsupportcafe.com
Subway C, E (Spring St) or 6 (Spring St)

| MON-FRI. | 7:00am - 8:00pm |
| SAT-SUN. | 8:00am - 8:00pm |

First opened 2009
Roaster Ground Support Coffee
Machine La Marzocco Linea
Grinder Mahlkönig EK 43, Mazzer Luigi Robur E

Espresso	$3.25
Cappuccino	$4.25
Latte	$4.25

MAP REF. **34**

COFFEE 4.25 / 5   OVERALL 4.25 / 5 ★★★★☆

Happy Bones

TOP 35

394 Broome Street, Manhattan, NY 10013 | **Nolita**

This shop used to be a walk-in refrigerator, if you can believe it, and before that, an alleyway. But with some imaginative design, it's become a fashionable café instead. Happy Bones is a neighborhood favorite, popular for flat whites and long blacks, drinks made popular since jumping over from Australia and New Zealand. The definite space is both industrial and elegant in feel, the white palette creates an excellent space for clearing your thoughts. Happy Bones sports only a few tables, but it's a beautiful spot to grab a drink before exploring the neighborhood.

(212) 673-3754
www.happybonesnyc.com
Subway 4, 6 (Spring St)

| MON-FRI. | 7:30am - 7:00pm |
| SAT-SUN. | 8:00am - 7:00pm |

First opened 2013
Roaster Counter Culture Coffee
Machine La Marzocco FB80
Grinder Mazzer Luigi

Espresso	$3.00
Cappuccino	$4.00
Latte	$4.50

MAP REF. **35**

COFFEE 4.50 / 5   OVERALL 4.50 / 5 ★★★★☆

Housing Works Bookstore Cafe

126 Crosby Street, Manhattan, NY 10012 | **Soho**

Photo courtesy of the venue

This Soho bookstore café serves up great coffee for a great cause. The Housing Works Organization is a non-profit that works to combat AIDs and homelessness through advocacy, services, and its businesses. As it is run by volunteers, one hundred percent of the proceeds from the bookstore and the café go toward Housing Works' mission. The café serves well-prepared Intelligentsia beans alongside baked goods and freshly made sandwiches. With spacious and comfortable seating, it's the perfect spot to curl up with great read or meet with friends for lunch, all for an amazing cause.

(212) 334-3324
www.housingworks.org/social-enterprise/bookstore-cafe

Subway B, D, F, M (Broadway - Lafayette St) or 4, 6 (Bleeker St)

MON-FRI.	9:00am - 9:00pm
SAT-SUN.	9:00am - 5:00pm

First opened 1996
Roaster Intelligentsia Coffee
Machine La Marzocco Linea, 2 groups
Grinder Mazzer Luigi Major

Espresso	$2.50
Cappuccino	$4.00
Latte	$4.00

MAP REF. **36**

COFFEE 4.00 / 5

OVERALL 4.00 / 5

Joe & The Juice

161 Prince Street, Manhattan, NY 10036 | **Soho**

With its dim lighting and loud dance music, this spacious New York outpost of the popular Danish coffee-and-juice bar feels more night club than café at times. However, that doesn't affect Joe & The Juice's regulars from stopping by to do some work. Alongside your caffeine kick, make sure to try one of their many delicious smoothies for a burst of healthy flavor.

(917) 565-4016
www.jocjuice.com
Subway C, E (Spring St)

MON-FRI.	6:00am - 8:00pm
SAT-SUN.	8:00am - 8:00pm

First opened 2016
Roaster Bewleys
Machine La Marzocco GB5, 3 groups
Grinder Nuova Simonelli Mythos

Espresso	$2.75
Cappuccino	$3.50
Latte	$2.75 / $3.75

MAP REF. **37**

COFFEE 4.00 / 5	🫘🫘🫘🫘🫘	OVERALL 4.25 / 5	★★★★✰

42

McNally Jackson Café

52 Prince Street, Manhattan, NY 10012 | **Noho**

Literary lovers will fall head over heels for this charming café on the ground floor of McNally Jackson, one of the city's most popular independent bookstores. This cozy space effortlessly blends coffee and culture. Stumptown coffee is proudly served, along with a selection of fair trade teas and light fare. It's the perfect spot to start that new book you've been dying to read, and an inspiring location for writers and other creatives to do some work.

(212) 274-1160
www.mcnallyjackson.com/cafe
Subway 4, 6 (Spring St) or N, R (Prince St) or B, D, F, M (Broadway - Lafayette St)

MON-SAT.	10:00am - 10:00pm
SUN.	10:00am - 9:00pm

First opened 2004
Roaster Stumptown Coffee Roasters
Machine La Marzocco Linea, 2 groups
Grinder Mazzer Luigi

Espresso	$2.75
Cappuccino	$3.50
Latte	$3.75 / $4.00

MAP REF. **38**

COFFEE 4.00 / 5	OVERALL 4.00 / 5

Nolita Mart & Espresso Bar

156 Mott Street, Manhattan, NY 10013 | **Chinatown**

Hidden in the middle of Chinatown is Nolita Mart, a calming surprise amidst the bustle of Grand Street. It's a unique space: coffee shop in the front, full grocery market in the back. Pop in for an excellent cup of Stumptown espresso, or if espresso isn't your style, they have a selection of hand poured options as well. Barstools in the front create a small seating area, separating the coffee from the market in the back. On a hot summer day, their cold brew is a welcome treat.

(212) 966-8883
www.nolitamart.com
Subway B, D (Grand St)

MON-FRI.	8:00am - 7:00pm
SAT-SUN.	8:30am - 7:00pm

First opened 2011
Roaster Stumptown Coffee Roasters
Machine La Marzocco GB5, 2 groups
Grinder Mazzer Luigi Kony E

Espresso	$3.25
Cappuccino	$4.00
Latte	$4.25

MAP REF. **39**

COFFEE 4.00 / 5	OVERALL 3.75 / 5

Saturdays Surf NYC

31 Crosby Street, Manhattan, NY 10013 | **Soho**

Many stores in Manhattan now happen to serve nice coffee, but Saturdays Surf feels like a genuine coffee shop which happens to also be a surf apparel store. This is mostly thanks to a gobsmackingly beautiful, spacious reclaimed-wood backyard, full of tulips, and the fact that it's staffed by folks who truly seem about to go for a surf. La Colombe makes a special blend for their drip, delicious and complex. And on a hot summers day when you might prefer to go for a surf, order a hot black coffee and lounge in the backyard, one of the most pleasant outdoor areas in Manhattan.

(212) 966-7875
www.saturdaysnyc.com
Subway 4, 6 (Canal St)

Sister locations West Village

MON–FRI.	8:00am – 7:00pm
SAT–SUN.	10:00am – 7:00pm

First opened 2009
Roaster La Colombe Torrefaction Coffee Roasters
Machine La Marzocco Linea, 3 groups
Grinder Mazzer Luigi

Espresso	$3.00
Cappuccino	$4.00
Latte	$4.00

MAP REF. **40**

COFFEE 4.00 / 5	🔵🔵🔵🔵⚪	OVERALL 4.25 / 5	★★★★⯪

Two Hands Soho

164 Mott Street, Manhattan, NY 10013 | **Soho**

TOP 35

The laidback attitude at this Aussie-run shop is more than welcome in this busy neighborhood. They've got a full menu of food with favorites like avocado toast and acai bowls and though the flat white reigns here, all their coffee drinks are good and strong, made with delicious Café Integral coffee. The space is bright and airy with its pristinely white interior and accents of greenery. This is a neighborhood favorite that gets packed on the weekends and weekdays, so hang with other coffee lovers and ride the wave over to this buzzing spot.

www.twohandsnyc.com
Subway B, D (Grand St)

Sister locations Tribeca

MON–SUN. 8:00am - 6:00pm

First opened 2014
Roaster Café Integral
Machine La Marzocco Strada, 2 groups
Grinder Compak F8

Espresso $3.00
Cappuccino $4.00
Latte $4.50

MAP REF. 41

COFFEE 4.50 / 5	OVERALL 4.50 / 5

CHEMEX

CELEBRATING 75 YEARS OF PERFECT EXTRACTION

The Chemex coffeemaker is recognized as an iconic piece of design history. This beautiful brewer, used in combination with our double bonded filter paper will extract the purest, most flavorful cup of coffee, every time.

follow @the_chemex ✕ chemexcoffeemaker.com

West Village & Neighboring

Known as 'The Village' to locals, Greenwich village houses some of the most expensive homes in Manhattan. With the area a landmark for bohemian culture, the desirable location is very sought after. Washington Square park is at the center of the neighborhood and provides much needed green space amongst the packed residential quarters. Nestled in the unique streets of the West Village lie many trendy food and coffee spots which offer a local vibe.

Bluestone Lane West Village

30 Carmine Street, Manhattan, NY 10014 | **West Village**

Photo: Ben Hider

The table service at this West Village branch of Bluestone couldn't be sweeter. And the café itself is gleaming with white walls, pale wood flooring and large windows letting in lots of light. The menu features fine Aussie brunch fare including eggs, avocados and sourdough, with several gluten-free offerings. It's easy to linger with friends - having no WiFi means that people actually talk to each other. For something different in your cup, try the "Magic": a double ristretto in a 4.5-ounce cup with steamed and micro-foamed milk.

(212) 627-2763
www.bluestonelaneny.com
Subway A, C, E, B, D, F, M (West 4th St)

Sister locations Greenwich Village / Upper East Side

MON–SUN. 8:00am - 6:00pm

First opened 2016
Roaster Bluestone Lane, Niccolo
Machine La Marzocco Linea, 3 groups
Grinder Nuova Simonelli Mythos

Espresso	$2.75
Cappuccino	$4.00
Latte	$4.00

MAP REF. 42

COFFEE 4.50 / 5	OVERALL 4.25 / 5

49

Bluestone Lane Greenwich Village

55 Greenwich Avenue, Manhattan, NY 10014 | **Greenwich Village**

Photo: Ben Hider

West Village & Neighboring

Bluestone Lane does not do unattractive: all its locations are a treat for the eye. But the Collective Café is particularly pretty, especially on a sunny day. The white picket fence might make you think you're in Melbourne or Sydney. The menu will do the same trick, with its Antipodean views of clean and healthy living (including a totally delectable brunch menu). Coffee at Bluestone is never anything less than outstanding: it's just a question of whether you're in the mood for a well-pulled espresso shot or a famous flat white.

(646) 368-1988
www.bluestonelaneny.com
Subway 1, 2 (Christopher St - Sheridan Sq) or 1, 2, 3 (14th St)

MON–SUN. 8:00am - 6:00pm

First opened 2014
Roaster Bluestone Lane, Niccolo
Machine La Marzocco Linea PB, 3 groups
Grinder Nuova Simonelli Mythos

Espresso	$2.75
Cappuccino	$4.00
Latte	$4.00

Sister locations Upper East Side / West Village

MAP REF. **43**

COFFEE 4.50 / 5	OVERALL 4.50 / 5

Chalait

224 West 4th Street, Manhattan, NY 10014 | **Greenwich Village**

Photo courtesy of the venue

Chalait calls itself a matcha/tea/coffee bar, and tea drinks do outnumber coffee on the list. Counter Culture coffee is made expertly here, and presented with care that befits the stylish surroundings. Chalait is a fantastically good-looking space, with huge windows on two sides and street-facing counters that allow for easy people-watching. There's seating for only fifteen, so it's hard to grab a spot at mealtimes, but worth the effort if you want to dig into delicious tartines and sandwiches.

(212) 929 0266
www.chalait.com
Subway 1, 2 (Christopher St Sheridan Sq)

MON–FRI. 7:00am - 7:00pm
SAT–SUN. 8:00am - 7:00pm

First opened 2015
Roaster Counter Culture Coffee
Machine La Marzocco Linea, 2 groups
Grinder Mazzer Luigi Robur

Espresso	$3.00
Cappuccino	$3.75
Latte	$4.50

MAP REF. **44**

West Village & Neighboring

COFFEE 4.25 / 5

OVERALL 4.50 / 5

51

The Coffee Foundry

186 West 4th Street, Manhattan, NY 10014 | **West Village**

Looking for a workplace coffee spot? The Coffee Foundry is for you. There are electrical outlets under the concrete counter, and meetings take place at the tables and in rentable rooms at the back of the industrial-looking space. Creative juices flow with expertly brewed cups using beans from Toby's Estate, bright and sprightly in the cup. While the food offering is small, it does include poké, Hawaii's signature raw-fish dish. But it isn't all work-work-work at this Foundry. There's an impressive sound system behind the bar. When the sun goes down, the cocktails come out and karaoke cranks up.

www.coffeefoundry.net
Subway A, C, E, B, D, F, M (West 4th St)

MON-FRI.	7:00am - 6:00pm
SAT.	10:00am - 5.30pm
SUN.	Closed

First opened 2010
Roaster Toby's Estate Coffee
Machine La Marzocco Strada, 2 groups
Grinder Ditting, Mazzer Luigi Super Jolly

Espresso	$3.00
Cappuccino	$3.50
Latte	$4.00

Sister locations Murray Hill   MAP REF. **45**

COFFEE 4.25 / 5	OVERALL 4.00 / 5 ★★★★☆

Fair Folks & a Goat

96 West Houston Street, Manhattan, NY 10012 | **Greenwich Village**

Fair Folks is a retailer of clothes, jewelry and accessories. But you'd be foolish not to turn left and address yourself to the barista. The clothes look as good as the coffees, with fine latte art adorning well-pulled shots using beans from the venerable Porto Rico roasters in the Village. A diverse set of local coffee drinkers and apparel shoppers puts the surprisingly light-filled room to good use, with some drawn by the membership deal: $35 a month buys you free drinks and discounts on other items. Doesn't that seem fair, folks?

(212) 420-7900
www.fairfolksandagoat.com
Subway B, D, F, M (Broadway - Lafayette St)

Sister locations East Village

MON-THU.	7:00am - 8:00pm
FRI.	7:00am - 9:00pm
SAT-SUN.	8:00am - 9:00pm

First opened 2012
Roaster Porto Rico Coffee Roasters
Machine Rancilio
Grinder Mazzer Luigi

Espresso	$2.50
Cappuccino	$3.50
Latte	$4.00

MAP REF. **46**

COFFEE 4.00 / 5	OVERALL 4.00 / 5 ★★★★☆

Jack's Stir Brew Coffee

138 West 10th Street, Manhattan, NY 10014 | **West Village**

Established in 2003, Jack's is an old school favorite amongst the NYC coffee scene. Photographs cover the walls of their 10th Street café, giving it a homey atmosphere. It is quiet and serene, the perfect spot to do work or just relax with a great cup of coffee. Community is emphasized at Jack's, baristas know a regular's order as soon as they step up to the counter. Pair your coffee with one of their delicious vegan baked goods, or take a bar of chocolate to-go.

(212) 929-0821
www.jacksstirbrew.com
Subway 1, 2 (Christopher St Sheridan Sq)

MON-FRI.	6:30am - 7:00pm
SAT-SUN.	7:00am - 7:00pm

First opened 2003
Roaster Jack's Stir Brew Roast
Machine La Marzocco GB5
Grinder Mazzer Luigi

Espresso	$2.73
Cappuccino	$4.00 / $4.50
Latte	$4.00 / $4.50

MAP REF. **47**

COFFEE 4.25 / 5 ● ● ● ● ◗   OVERALL 4.25 / 5 ★ ★ ★ ★ ☆

Kava Cafe

803 Washington Street, Manhattan, NY 10014 | **West Village**

This polished coffee bar pulls excellent shots on their sleek La Marzocco Strada, and the filter coffee is notable. With a typical Italian inspired interior and coffee to match this Washington Street café is true Italian. If you are after something other than coffee then give the beer a try.

(212) 255-7495
www.kavanyc.com
Subway L (8th Avenue) or A, C, E (14th Street)

MON-WED.	7:00am - 7:00pm
THU-FRI.	7:00am - 9:00pm
SAT.	8:00am - 9:00pm
SUN.	8:00am - 7:00pm

First opened 2011
Roaster Ceremony
Machine La Marzocco Strada
Grinder Mazzer Luigi

Espresso	$3.50
Cappuccino	$4.50
Latte	$5.00

MAP REF. **48**

COFFEE 4.25 / 5 ● ● ● ● ◗   OVERALL 4.25 / 5 ★ ★ ★ ★ ☆

Kobrick Coffee Co.

24 9th Avenue, Manhattan, NY 10014 | **West Village**

After roasting beans for nearly a century, Kobrick decided to open a café in the trendy meatpacking in 2015. Yet it feels as if it might have been there forever, with its tasteful and timeless dark wood décor (look up at the ceiling) and deeply comfortable gentleman's-club-type seating in the small back room. Kobrick makes incredibly good coffee, whether espresso or drip. Food is simple, like the room: eggs, sandwiches, boards of charcuterie and cheeses are served here. The place is open late, with coffee joined by cocktails as the drinks of choice. Kobrick is a little piece of Old Manhattan on Ninth Avenue - more 1920 than 20-whatever.

(212) 255-5588
www.kobricks.com
Subway A, C, E (14th St)

MON-FRI.	7:00am - 2:00am
SAT-SUN.	8:00am - 2:00am

First opened 2015
Roaster Kobrick Coffee Co.
Machine La Marzocco GB5, 3 groups
Grinder Mahlkönig K30 Espresso, Mahlkönig Guatemala

Espresso	$3.25
Cappuccino	$4.00
Latte	$4.00

MAP REF. **49**

COFFEE 4.25 / 5

OVERALL 4.25 / 5 ★★★★☆

54

Porto Rico Importing Co.

201 Bleeker Street, Manhattan, NY 10012 | **Greenwich Village**

Photo courtesy of the venue

Porto Rico is truly a coffee emporium, offering a comprehensive selection of direct-trade beans imported from around the world. Established in 1907, this family-owned coffee store has been passed down through the generations, gathering a loyal following throughout the years. Though not a café, head to the coffee bar in the back, where a friendly barista will gladly pour a brew for you. No matter your taste, Porto Rico offers a blend for everyone, as well as selling quality machinery to get the most out of their flavor-filled beans.

(212) 477-5421
www.portorico.com
Subway 1, 2 (Houston St) or A, C, E (Spring St)

Sister location East Village / Lower East Side / Williamsburg

MON-FRI.	8:00am - 9:00pm
SAT.	9:00am - 9:00pm
SUN.	12:00pm - 7:00pm

First opened 1907
Roaster Porto Rico Coffee Roasters
Machine Astoria SEP Perla, 2 groups
Grinder Mahlkönig

Espresso	$1.60
Cappuccino	$3.25
Latte	$3.25

MAP REF. **50**

COFFEE 4.00 / 5 🫘🫘🫘🫘🫘

OVERALL 4.25 / 5 ★★★★☆

55

Prodigy Coffee

33 Carmine Street, Manhattan, NY 10014 | **Greenwich Village**

Prodigy Coffee uses its own roaster to prepare exceptional traditional coffees and their own specially concocted drinks too. When it's hot try the Frostbite, cold brew over shaved ice, or maybe the Snakebite, melted dark chocolate with a shot of espresso, when the weather cools down. With these potions, and their family of seasonal single origins and blends, it's easy to have fun experimenting with your taste of coffee here. The six table shop is handsome, with gilded frames and chandeliers composing the space with a polished flare.

(212) 414-4142
www.prodigycoffee.com
Subway A, C, E, B, D, F, M (West 4th St)

MON–FRI.	7:00am – 7:00pm
SAT–SUN.	8:00am – 7:00pm

First opened 2012
Roaster Gotham Coffee Roasters
Machine La Marzocco Linea, 2 groups
Grinder Mazzer Luigi Robur, Kony

Espresso	$3.25
Cappuccino	$4.00
Latte	$4.25

MAP REF. 51

Stumptown Greenwich Village

30 West 8th Street, Manhattan, NY 10011 | **Greenwich Village**

West Village & Neighboring

Stumptown found a new home here in 2013, bringing its signature Portland style and meticulously prepared coffees downtown. This former village bookshop now houses Stumptown's library of perfectly prepared coffees. The delicious Nitro cold brew is served on tap, with a strong dark and creamy taste reminiscent of a nice Guinness. There's an adjoining brew bar where you can get any coffee made any way you like, and they play kind hosts with regular tastings there too.

(855) 711-3385
www.stumptowncoffee.com
Subway N, R (8th St - NYU)

Sister locations Midtown West

MON-SUN. 7:00am - 8:00pm

First opened 2013
Roaster Stumptown Coffee Roasters
Machine La Marzocco Strada
Grinder Mazzer Luigi Robur E

Espresso $3.25
Cappuccino $4.00
Latte $4.00 / $4.50 / $5.00

MAP REF. **52**

COFFEE 4.75 / 5

OVERALL 4.50 / 5 ★★★★⯨

Third Rail Coffee

240 Sullivan Street, Manhattan, NY 10012 | **Greenwich Village**

Despite being tiny, Third Rail is a comfortable place to sip your coffee, thanks to the genuine, relaxed warmth of the baristas. They always serve ethics-focused, consistently great Counter Culture Coffee beans, complete with exquisite latte art on milky brews, but also rotate a second roaster for pour-overs (at the time of writing, Sweetbloom from Denver). The lattes are excellent, but if you have time, stay for a pour-over.

(646) 580-1240
www.thirdrailcoffee.com
Subway A, C, E, B, D, F, M (W. 4th St)

Sister locations East Village

MON-FRI.	7:00am - 8:00pm
SAT-SUN.	8:00am - 8:00pm

First opened 2009
Roaster Counter Culture Coffee and guests
Machine La Marzocco GB5, 2 groups
Grinder Mazzer Luigi Robur E

Espresso	$3.25
Cappuccino	$4.00
Latte	$4.00 / $4.50

MAP REF. **53**

COFFEE 4.50 / 5	⬤⬤⬤⬤◗	OVERALL 4.25 / 5	★★★★✩

Toby's Estate West Village

44 Charles Street, Manhattan, NY 10014 | **West Village**

TOP 35

West Village & Neighboring

Toby's West Village location began life as an artist's studio almost a century ago, and there are huge windows on two sides of the V-shaped room. Combined with high ceilings, this creates an airy and spacious feel - and a great setting for digging in to their excellent baked goods from highest quality suppliers, including Ovenly, or relaxing over breakfast of eggs or granola. The pour-over coffees are outstanding, and showcase the roasting skill at Toby's Brooklyn base. If you crave caffeine enlightenment, go to one of their classes in the training lab downstairs.

(646) 590-1924
www.tobysestate.com
Subway 1 (Christopher St - Sheridan Sq)

Sister locations Flatiron / Midtown East / Williamsburg

MON-SUN.   7:00am - 7:00pm

First opened 2014
Roaster Toby's Estate Coffee
Machine La Marzocco Strada, 2 groups
Grinder Nuova Simonelli Mythos One

Espresso	$3.00
Cappuccino	$3.75
Latte	$4.50

MAP REF. 54

COFFEE 4.50 / 5   🫘🫘🫘🫘🫘

OVERALL 4.50 / 5   ★★★★★

Chelsea

Running along the Hudson River, Chelsea is home to the popular green oasis of The Highline, the historic Chelsea Piers, bustling Chelsea Market and busy Hudson Yards. With these fantastic areas offering residents a variety of local charms it's easy to see why Chelsea is one of Manhattan's hotspots. Featuring some of the best dinning, nightlife and art galleries in Manhattan, Chelsea is a definite neighborhood to visit.

Blue Bottle Chelsea

450 West 15th Street, Manhattan, NY 10014 | **Chelsea**

Photo courtesy of the venue

This pocket-size branch of the San Francisco-based chain is perfectly situated for visits to Chelsea Market or the High Line. The space, originally a loading dock, is cleverly used: the café is at street level, while the rear mezzanine accommodates Saturday classes (free of charge) in cupping and home brewing. Blue Bottle roasts at its flagship Williamsburg site, and the beans include both blends and single origins. Whether pulled through the three-group Strada or lovingly hand-poured, the coffee is treated like royalty. Blue Bottle is blue chip all the way, right down to its delectable in-house baking.

(510) 653-3394
bluebottlecoffee.com
Subway A, C, E (14th St)

MON–FRI.	7:00am – 6:00pm
SAT–SUN.	8:00am – 6:00pm

First opened 2012
Roaster Blue Bottle Coffee
Machine La Marzocco Strada, 3 groups
Grinder Mazzer Luigi, Baratza Forte

Espresso	$3.00
Cappuccino	$4.00
Latte	$4.50

Sister locations Bryant Park / Cobble Hill / Hell's Kitchen / High Line / Met Breuer / Rockefeller Center / Williamsburg

MAP REF. 55

COFFEE 4.50 / 5	OVERALL 4.25 / 5

The Commons Chelsea

128th 7th Avenue, Manhattan, NY 10014 | **Chelsea**

Photo courtesy of the venue

The terrific beans from La Colombe get excellent care in this small, very calm Chelsea local. It places strong emphasis on food, served from breakfast onward through dinner, when you can relax with beer or wine as well as coffee. The owners were the first people selling on the High Line, so they're West Side veterans. Tables outside are a great place to perch in fine weather; and latte art can reach some pretty impressive heights. A remarkable venue.

(212) 929-9333
www.thecommonschelsea.com
Subway A, C, E (14th St)

MON-FRI.	7:00am - 11:00pm
SAT-SUN.	9:00am - 6:00pm

First opened 2011
Roaster La Colombe Coffee Roasters
Machine La Marzocco Linea, 2 groups
Grinder Mazzer Luigi Super Jolly

Espresso	$3.00 / $3.50
Cappuccino	$4.00 / $4.75
Latte	$4.00 / $4.75

MAP REF. 56

COFFEE 4.00 / 5   OVERALL 4.25 / 5 ★★★★☆

Intelligentsia Coffee

180 10th Avenue, Manhattan, NY 10011 | **Chelsea**

This Chicago behemoth has made a home inside the elegant lobby of the High Line Hotel. 'Twas the night before Christmas' was written in an apple orchard that once grew upon these historic grounds, and now you too can wax poetic here with an exceptional coffee in hand. The menu changes often with seasonal offerings and they feature a slow bar in lieu of filter coffee where single origins are brewed with care. We suggest drinking al fresco, as the hotel offers beautiful outdoor spaces where coffee patrons can relax in style.

(212) 933-9736
www.intelligentsiacoffee.com
Subway C, E (23rd St)

SUN-THU. 7:00am - 6:00pm
FRI-SAT. 7:00am - 7:00pm

First opened 2013
Roaster Intelligentsia Coffee
Machine La Marzocco Strada, 2 groups
Grinder Mazzer Luigi Robur

Espresso $3.25
Cappuccino $4.25
Latte $4.50

MAP REF. 57

COFFEE 4.50 / 5 | **OVERALL** 4.50 / 5 ★★★★✦

65

Joe Coffee Pro Shop + HQ

131 West 21st Street, Manhattan, NY 10011 | **Flatiron**

Chelsea

There isn't much seating at Joe Pro's Flatiron shop, but it's probably not needed as most people seem to come in for something to drink on the go. In spite of its size, it's worth coming in to drink on the premises. This is where Joe does his roasting, an operation you can watch behind the glass panels. And while you're watching, you can talk to your heart's content with baristas who are as eager and as knowledgeable as any in the city. While you're there, stock up on beans.

(212) 924-7400
www.joenewyork.com
Subway 1, 2 (23rd St)

Sister locations Joe - Upper East Side

MON-FRI.	8:00am - 6:00pm
SAT-SUN.	9:00am - 4:00pm

First opened 2012
Roaster Joe and guests
Machine La Marzocco Strada, 2 groups
Grinder Mazzer Luigi Robur E, Mahlkönig EK 43

Espresso	$3.00
Cappuccino	$4.00
Latte	$4.50

MAP REF. **58**

COFFEE 4.25 / 5

OVERALL 4.25 / 5 ★★★★☆

66

MatchaBar Chelsea

256 West 15th Street, Manhattan, NY 10011 | **Chelsea**

This Chelsea outpost of MatchaBar proves the proposition that good things come in small packages. The place is so pint-sized it needs just a one-group machine, a real rarity. Set in a quiet residential block just east of 8th Avenue, MatchaBar Chelsea has space for just a handful of drinkers, with a large proportion of business coming from those on the go. Like the Williamsburg original, the espresso machine, a Simonelli, is operated with skill, making the bracing Toby's Estate espresso blend, in addition to the matcha, a lively base for skilled latte art. And here too, goods are the star turn on the food counter.

(212) 627-1058
www.matchabarnyc.com
Subway A, C, E, L (14th St)

Sister locations Williamsburg

MON-FRI.	8:00am - 7:00pm
SAT-SUN.	10:00am - 7:00pm

First opened 2015
Roaster Toby's Estate Coffee
Machine Nuova Simonelli, 1 group
Grinder Cuisinart

Espresso	$3.00
Cappuccino	$4.50
Latte	$4.85

MAP REF. 59

COFFEE 4.00 / 5 🫘🫘🫘🫘🫘

OVERALL 4.00 / 5 ★★★★★

Seven Grams Caffé

275 7th Avenue, Manhattan, NY 10001 | **Chelsea**

Photo courtesy of the venue

Seven Grams punches way above its weight through an enviable combination of great looks (including white walls hung with interesting art), eager service, and delicious baked goods all made in-house. It would be worth coming here even if the place didn't sell such good coffee - but the coffee is great, small doses of ground Fairtrade beans crowned with latte art that's inventive and highly skilled. Chelsea may have lots of other coffee spots to visit, but you should consider tipping the scales in favor of a visit to this one.

(212) 727-1777
www.sevengramscaffe.com
Subway 1, 2, F, M, A, C, E (23rd St)

MON-FRI. 7:00am - 7:00pm
SAT-SUN. 8:00am - 7:00pm

First opened 2015
Roaster La Colombe Coffee Roasters
Machine La Marzocco GB5
Grinder Nuova Simonelli

Espresso	$2.50
Cappuccino	$4.00
Latte	$4.00

MAP REF. **60**

COFFEE 4.25 / 5

OVERALL 4.50 / 5 ★★★★⯪

Think Coffee

500 West 30th Street, Manhattan, NY 10001 | **Chelsea**

Think's consistent high quality continues in this newest outpost, but the setting is unusual. It's on the edge of the Hudson Yards development. The entrance to the Holland Tunnel isn't far away. But Think makes its own charm with a smallish, colourful interior with nice glass panelling, a friendly crew, and excellent coffee; check out their killer drip and multitude of well-crafted espresso-based drinks. With the Abington Towers apartment building now open, and the High Line a few minutes away, Think is already popular. When Hudson Yards opens up, think: heaving.

(646) 649-4053
www.thinkcoffeenyc.com
Subway 7 (34th St - Hudson Yards)

Sister locations 8 New York venues

MON-FRI.	6:30am - 8:00pm
SAT-SUN.	7:30am - 8:00pm

First opened 2015
Roaster Red House
Machine Synesso Hydra, 3 groups
Grinder Mahlkönig Guatemala, Mazzer Luigi Robur E

Espresso	$2.75
Cappuccino	$3.85
Latte	$3.85

MAP REF. **61**

COFFEE 4.25 / 5

OVERALL 4.25 / 5

Underline Coffee

511 West 20th Street, Manhattan, NY 10011 | **Chelsea**

Photo courtesy of the venue

The "line" they refer to in the title of this cool, artisan shop is of course the Highline, the beautiful elevated park that runs over this great little café. Classic tunes play throughout this chilled, but serious coffee shop, as their handsome menus dutifully describe and explain the plenitude of offers they have on the bar. They use Apes & Peacocks for house-made speciality drinks and keep a slow bar going with single origins made to order, with both a blend and seasonal option available for espresso too.

(917) 447-9476
underlinecoffee.com
Subway C, E (23rd St)

MON–SAT.	7:00am – 7:00pm
SUN.	9.00am – 6.00pm

First opened 2014
Roaster Apes & Peacocks
Machine Kees Van Der Westen Mirage Idrocompresso, 2 group
Grinder Compak K10, Mahlkönig EK 43

Espresso	$3.00
Cappuccino	$3.75
Latte	$4.25

MAP REF. **62**

Chelsea

COFFEE 4.25 / 5

OVERALL 4.25 / 5 ★★★★⯪

70

Chalait

Midtown & Gramercy

Midtown is fast-paced, bustling and one of the greatest commercial centers in the world. The Empire State Building, The New York Public Library, MoMA and the core of New York's theatre district - including the bright lights of Times Square - can all be found in Midtown. This area is also home to the small and elegant Gramercy, a quiet neighborhood with the private, preserved Gramercy Park at its center: a lovely reminder of New York's Victorian history.

Birch Coffee Flatiron District

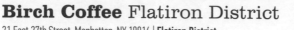

21 East 27th Street, Manhattan, NY 10016 | **Flatiron District**

Birch Coffee has made a cozy home at this end of 27th Street, with its assertively charming belief that coffee can and should bring people together. The shop has an "Ignition Initiative" with its collection of conversation starters that they suggest people enjoy with a neighbor. Their deeply satisfying own blend coffees make for lovely treats to share with old and new friends alike.

(212) 686-1444
www.birchcoffee.com
Subway N, Q, R (28th St)

Sister locations Financial District / Long Island City / Murray Hill / Upper East / Upper West / West Village

MON-SUN. 7:00am - 8:00pm

First opened 2009
Roaster Birch Coffee Roasters
Machine La Marzocco Strada
Grinder Mahlkönig, Mazzer Luigi Robur

Espresso	$3.00 / $4.00	
Cappuccino	$3.00 / $4.00	
Latte	$3.00 / $4.00	

MAP REF. **63**

COFFEE 4.50 / 5

OVERALL 4.50 / 5 ★★★★⯪

Brooklyn Roasting Company

Flatiron District 50 West 23rd Street, Manhattan, NY 10010 | **Flatiron**

Photo courtesy of the venue

While Brooklyn's flagship Navy Yard roastery/café embraces its industrial origins, this Flatiron space is much more Manhattan-slick, with checked floor tiles and soothing cream paint on the walls and ceiling. It's a big place, and needs to be: Brooklyn's well-deserved reputation for great coffee (single-origin drip is always sensational) and good food draws in crowds so big they need a rope barrier to keep them orderly. There's a nice mix of office workers and hipster aficionados here.

(718) 412-0080
www.brooklynroasting.com
Subway F, M (23rd St)

Sister locations Dumbo / Navy Yard

MON-SUN. 7:00am - 7:00pm

First opened 2015
Roaster Brooklyn Roasting Company
Machine La Marzocco Linea GB5, 2 groups
Grinder Nuova Simonelli Mythos One

Espresso	$2.50
Cappuccino	$3.75
Latte	$4.50

MAP REF. **64**

COFFEE 4.25 / 5 OVERALL 4.00 / 5 ★★★★★

74

Café Grumpy Grand Central Terminal

89 East 42nd Street, Manhattan, NY 10017 | **Midtown East**

Photo: Brad Chaffin

Café Grumpy's Grand Central outlet has loads of competitors for your brew-time buck, but it offers something special: a small, attractive space with a window onto Lexington Avenue. It feels like a real café rather than a mass-transit pit stop. Despite the size you may have luck getting a seat, because so much of the trade is takeout. Carry your beautifully crafted latte to a table and sit down to read The New Yorker, or just look out the window. GCT is all hustle and bustle, but Grumpy is all sip and chill.

(212) 661-2198
www.cafegrumpy.com
Subway 6 (51st St)

Sister locations Chelsea / Greenpoint / Lower East Side / Midtown / Park Slope

MON-FRI.	6:00am - 8:00pm
SAT-SUN.	7:00am - 8:00pm

First opened 2014
Roaster Café Grumpy Coffee
Machine Synesso
Grinder Nuova Simonelli Mythos, Mazzer Luigi Robur E

Espresso	$3.00
Cappuccino	$4.00
Latte	$4.50

MAP REF. **65**

COFFEE 4.25 / 5	🫘🫘🫘🫘🫘	OVERALL 4.00 / 5	★★★★★

Cafe Tarantin

302 West 38th Street, Manhattan, NY 10018 | **Hell's Kitchen**

The warmth of the welcome is the first thing you notice at Café Tarantin. The second is the charming décor, emphasized by dark wood and a cool mirror adorning one wall of the small room. Across from it is the bar, from which cheerful staff dispense their drinks. Most people coming here have something to eat, and the pan-Mediterranean menu focuses big on sandwiches, salads and pasta. Most finish with coffee, which is well made using beans from the Arista roastery in Queens.

(212) 239-1921
Subway A, C, B, D & 1 (Columbus Circle)

MON-THU.	8:00am - 10:00pm
FRI.	8:00am - 4:30pm
SAT.	Closed
SUN.	10:00am - 4:00pm

First opened 2013
Roaster Arista Coffee
Machine La Marzocco Linea, 2 groups
Grinder Mazzer Luigi Super Jolly

Espresso	$2.75
Cappuccino	$3.75
Latte	$4.75

MAP REF. **66**

COFFEE 4.00 / 5   **OVERALL** 4.00 / 5   ★ ★ ★ ★ ☆

Culture 36

247 West 36th Street, Manhattan, NY 10018 | **Garment District**

The second Garment District outpost of Culture Espresso is true to its name: only espresso and its milky offspring are served. You won't be disappointed, because the baristas know what they're doing with their gleaming Synesso. The Heart blend is bright and bracing, easily good enough to drink without sugar. There's an original ceiling high overhead and one big table offering the bulk of the seating in the spacious room. They bake their own delicious chocolate chip cookies, and once you've had one, you'll keep coming back for more.

www.cultureespresso.com
Subway A, C, E (34th St-Penn Station)

Sister locations Culture Espresso Bar - Midtown West

MON-FRI.	7:00am - 7:00pm
SAT-SUN.	8:00am - 7:00pm

First opened 2015
Roaster Heart Coffee
Machine Synesso Hydra, 3 groups
Grinder Mazzer Luigi Robur E, Mahlkönig

Espresso	$3.00
Cappuccino	$4.00
Latte	$4.50

MAP REF. **67**

COFFEE 4.50 / 5   **OVERALL** 4.25 / 5   ★ ★ ★ ★ ☆

Culture Espresso

72 West 38th Street, Manhattan, NY 10018 | **Midtown West**

TOP 35

Years ago, Culture was pretty much the only place to get great coffee near 42nd Street. Even though that's no longer the case, Culture's relaxed California-tinged atmosphere - despite constant foot-traffic - makes it stand out. Besides Stumptown's impossibly creamy, must-try nitro cold-brew on draught, the beans are from the excellent Heart Roasters of Portland. The baristas know what they're doing here, and you can't go wrong, whether you order an espresso, macchiato, or flat white. There's just enough space to sit down and relax, as you watch Midtown race by.

(212) 302-0200
www.cultureespresso.com
Subway B, D, F, M (42nd St-Bryant Park)

Sister locations Culture 36 - Garment District

MON-FRI.	7:00am - 7:00pm
SAT-SUN.	8:00am - 7:00pm

First opened 2009
Roaster Heart Coffee Roasters
Machine La Marzocco Strada, 3 groups
Grinder Mazzer Luigi Robur E

Espresso	$3.00
Cappuccino	$4.50
Latte	$4.50

MAP REF. **68**

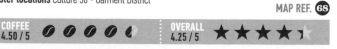

COFFEE 4.50 / 5

OVERALL 4.25 / 5 ★★★★⭑

Fika Tower & Bakery

824 10th Avenue, Manhattan, NY 10019 | **Hell's Kitchen**

Fika's 10th Avenue space is one of its best, with tall ceilings, white walls, copious light from the front windows and skylight, and discreet but distinctive decorative touches. This is a place to come and eat gorgeous Swedish-inspired food, with large platters a specialty. Of course, being Swedish, it does not neglect the sweet stuff either. There is a touch of berry sweetness in their well-made espresso, made with care and served with a smile. A great place to come after exploring the pier, just two blocks away.

(646) 490-7650
www.fikanyc.com
Subway 1, 2 (66th St - Lincoln Center)

Sister locations Multiple locations
in Manhattan

MON-FRI.	7:00am - 7:00pm
SAT-SUN.	9:00am - 7:00pm

First opened 2014
Roaster Fika
Machine Synesso Cyncra, 3 groups
Grinder Bunn

Espresso	$2.30
Cappuccino	$4.13
Latte	$4.36

MAP REF. **69**

COFFEE 4.00 / 5

OVERALL 4.50 / 5

78

Frisson Espresso

326 West 47th Street, Manhattan, NY 10036 | **Midtown West**

Owners Tulian Sanchez and Robert Melo have been friends since they were five, so it's not surprising that they work together well in running this peachy Theater District espresso spot. The place which sits around sixteen people, can be jumping any time of day, with a clientele they describe as "a little bit of everything,". Coffee is well made using beans from Dallis Bros. in Long Island City, and latte art is beautiful. Try to bag a table if you can and just sit back and enjoy the show.

(646) 850-3928
Subway 1, 2, A, C, E (50th St) or
N, Q, R (49th St)

MON–FRI.	7:00am - 7:00pm
SAT.	9:00am - 8:00pm
SUN.	9:00am - 6:00pm

First opened 2014
Roaster Dallis Bros. Coffee
Machine Synesso Cyncra, 3 groups
Grinder Compak E10

Espresso	$3.00
Cappuccino	$4.00
Latte	$4.50

MAP REF. **70**

COFFEE 4.00 / 5 — OVERALL 4.00 / 5 ★★★★☆

Ground Central Coffee Co. 2nd Avenue

800 2nd Avenue, Manhattan, NY 10013 | **Midtown East**

This small branch of Ground Central, the company's second, maintains a steady buzz thanks to two huge nearby suppliers of thirsty workers: Grand Central Station and the UN. It's not surprising that customers choose Ground Central, with coffee this good pouring steadily out of their machines. Single-origin drip and pour-over are outstanding, from a changing range. The espresso-based drinks feature latte art that could easily win professional competitions. No wonder Ground Central is almost as busy as Grand Central.

(646) 484-5697
www.ground-central.com
Subway 4, 5, 6 (Grand Central)

Sister locations Theater District / Lower Manhattan

MON–FRI.	6:30am - 7:00pm
SAT-SUN.	7:00am - 5:00pm

First opened 2015
Roaster La Colombe Coffee Roasters
Machine La Marzocco
Grinder Mazzer Luigi Super Jolly

Espresso	$2.95
Cappuccino	$3.95
Latte	$4.15 / $4.65

MAP REF. **71**

COFFEE 4.25 / 5 — OVERALL 4.00 / 5 ★★★★☆

Ground Central Coffee Co. 52nd Street

155 East 52nd Street, Manhattan, NY 10017 | **Midtown East**

This original branch of Ground Central feels more like a European-style café than a contemporary-style coffee place. It's sleek and elegant, and the prominence given to their serious sandwiches and enticing baked goods makes it clear that food plays a major role. Swap your coffee for a cocktail later in the day. A collection of vinyl discs lines a front wall, and the soundtrack favors timeless rock 'n' roll classics. The baristas rock their three-group Faema, too, but don't neglect the single-origin drip brews.

(646) 964-4438
www.ground-central.com
Subway E, M (Lexington Ave / 53rd St)

Sister locations Midtown East /
Lower Manhattan

MON-FRI.	6:30am - 9:00pm
SAT-SUN.	9:00am - 6:00pm

First opened 2014
Roaster La Colombe Coffee Roasters
Machine Faema E61, 3 groups
Grinder Mazzer Luigi Robur E

Espresso	$2.95
Cappuccino	$3.95
Latte	$4.15 / $4.65

MAP REF. **72**

COFFEE 4.25 / 5

OVERALL 4.00 / 5

Hole in the Wall

420 5th Avenue, Manhattan, NY 10018 | **Midtown West**

Photo courtesy of the venue

The name does not do this coffee bar justice, wriggled into the corner of a busy office building. It streamlines the morning dash, bringing fine coffee as close to the office as possible. But this smart shop's open to the public too! Enter around either corner of the building and grab a coffee to enjoy while you pound the streets. They also offer sandwiches (including the ever popular avocado toast) as well as fresh, locally baked goods like big, glorious doughnuts.

(646) 682-9510
www.holeinthewallnyc.com
Subway N, Q, R, B, D, F, M (34th St - Herald Square)

MON–FRI.	7:00am – 5:00pm
SAT–SUN.	Closed

First opened 2014
Roaster Novo
Machine Synesso
Grinder Mazzer Luigi

Espresso	$3.25
Cappuccino	$4.45
Latte	$4.90

MAP REF. **78**

COFFEE 4.00 / 5

OVERALL 4.00 / 5 ★★★★☆

Irving Farm Coffee Roasters

Gramercy 71 Irving Place, Manhattan, NY 10003 | **Gramercy**

TOP 35

Settled at the bottom of a brownstone on quiet Irving Place, Irving Farm is a New York City institution. The street may be serene, but step inside to find a café bustling with energy. There is a constant stream of people moving in and out of this cozy café, which can be a bit snug in terms of seating, but that is part of its charming atmosphere. The lights are low, the baristas are pros, and their coffee, which is roasted at their Hudson Valley roastery, is expertly brewed.

(212) 995-5252
www.irvingfarm.com
Subway N, R, W, 4, 5, 6, L (Union Square
- 14th St)

Sister locations Grand Central Terminal /
Lower East Side / Financial District / Upper
East Side / Upper West Side

MON–FRI.	7:00am - 10:00pm
SAT–SUN.	8:00am - 10:00pm

First opened 1996
Roaster Irving Farm Coffee Roasters
Machine La Marzocco Linea, 2 groups
Grinder Nuova Simonelli Mythos Clima Pro

Espresso	$3.25
Cappuccino	$4.25
Latte	$4.75

MAP REF. **74**

COFFEE 4.50 / 5   OVERALL 4.50 / 5 ★★★★✩

Kahve

667 10th Avenue, Manhattan, NY 10019 | **Hell's Kitchen**

The second incarnation of Kahve is brightly modern in décor and has much more seating space than the nearby original. It's a very good place to settle in for working, though the seats in the window make a good place for people-watching. In addition to the signature Kahve offerings of brewed coffee, espresso-based drinks, and indulgent latte tweaks, this branch serves nitro-brew from a tap on the counter. The baristas know their business, and they know how to smile, a winning combination from this rising star of New York's coffee scene.

(646) 649-4503
www.kahvenyc.com
Subway A, C, E (50th St)

Sister locations Hell's Kitchen

MON–FRI.	7:00am – 8:00pm
SAT.	7:30am – 8:00pm
SUN.	8:30am – 8:00pm

First opened 2016
Roaster Secret
Machine Nuova Simonelli Aurelia, 2 groups
Grinder Nuova Simonelli MDX

Espresso	$2.00
Cappuccino	$3.25
Latte	$3.25

MAP REF. 75

COFFEE 4.00 / 5

OVERALL 4.00 / 5 ★★★★☆

Le Café Coffee

7 East 14th Street, Manhattan, NY 10003 | **Gramercy**

Photo courtesy of the venue

Situated in the middle of the always hectic 14th Street, Le Café Coffee is an oasis from the Manhattan mayhem. It's small, but never too crowded, making it the perfect spot to take a seat and relax amidst the outside chaos. The service is refreshingly friendly, the conversation personalized as they prepare your order. They serve espresso-based beverages as well as drip alongside a small menu of fresh sandwiches. Additionally, there is a seasonal menu of specialty beverages, and their matcha latte is especially of note.

(212) 365-1060
www.lecafecoffee.com
Subway 4, 5,6, N, Q, R, L (14th St - Union Sq)

MON-THU.	7:00am - 8:30pm
FRI.	7:00am - 9:00pm
SAT.	8:00am - 9:00pm
SUN.	0:00am - 0:00pm

First opened 2013
Roaster La Colombe Coffee Roasters
Machine La Marzocco, 2 groups
Grinder Mazzer Luigi

Espresso	$2.75
Cappuccino	$3.75
Latte	$4.00

MAP REF. **76**

COFFEE 4.25 / 5　🫘🫘🫘🫘🫘

OVERALL 4.00 / 5　★★★★☆

84

Little Collins

667 Lexington Avenue, Manhattan, NY 10022 | **Midtown East**

Australian-influenced Little Collins is the civilized coffee shop the upper east side has always needed but didn't have until 2013. Focused, friendly baristas in old-fashioned uniforms work diligently and quickly to serve a constant stream of business people and yogis. If you're able to snag a stool, the staff make you feel at home, pouring you tap water without being asked to do so. The espresso, strong and delicious, comes with a tiny almond cookie, a nice touch. Single-origin pour-overs are made with a ModBar contraption which heats and pours the water-it's like having a robot hand-pour your coffee.

(212) 308-1969
www.littlecollinsnyc.com
Subway 4, 5, 6 (59th St - Lexington Ave)

MON-FRI.   7:00am - 5:00pm
SAT-SUN.   8:00am - 4:00pm

First opened 2013
Roaster Counter Culture Coffee
Machine ModBar
Grinder Mazzer Luigi Robur, Nuova Simonelli Mythos

Espresso $3.25
Cappuccino $4.00
Latte $4.25

MAP REF. **77**

COFFEE 4.50 / 5

OVERALL 4.50 / 5 ★★★★⯪

Ninth Street Espresso Midtown East

109 East 56th Street, Manhattan, NY 10022 | **Midtown East**

The Ninth Street Espresso menu boasts just 4 options, none of which are "cappuccino" or "latte" - instead, simply "espresso with milk". This minimalist touch is one of several ways it conveys it's serious about espresso, and their strong, viscous shots back that up. The timeless, black-and-white-tiled space, inside the swanky Lombardy hotel, has a few stools, but is more suited to the droves of businesspeople who line up to throw back a shot. If you can avoid feeling like a philistine in comparison, order the smooth, sweet cold-brew; it's the best in the city.

(646) 559-4793
www.ninthstreetespresso.com
Subway 4, 5, 6, N, Q, R (59th St)

MON-FRI.	7:00am - 7:00pm
SAT.-SUN.	8:00am - 5:00pm

First opened 2013
Roaster Ninth Street Espresso
Machine La Marzocco Linea
Grinder Grindmaster

Espresso $3.00

Sister locations Alphabet City / Chelsea / East Village

MAP REF. **78**

COFFEE 4.50 / 5	OVERALL 4.25 / 5

Oren's Daily Roast Midtown West

1440 Broadway, Manhattan, NY 10018 | **Midtown West**

Oren's does a brisk business for good reasons: the coffee is solid and the stores well run. At this branch, nearly everyone seems to come in for something to go. Single-origin brews, using beans bought directly from the producers, are the obvious choice for drinking on the move. This branch, one of Oren's nine locations in New York is right on the doorstep of the tourist-and-traffic magnet that is Times Square and 42nd Street, a welcome addition to this busy area.

(646) 291-2090
www.orensdailyroast.com
Subway B, D, F, M (42nd St - Bryant Park)

Sister locations 8 New York locations

MON-FRI.	7:00am - 7:00pm
SAT.	8:00am - 2:00pm
SUN.	Closed

First opened 2011
Roaster Oren's Daily Roast
Machine La Marzocco GB, 2 groups
Grinder Mazzer Luigi Robur E, Mahlkönig Guatemala Lab

Espresso $2.75
Cappuccino $3.60 / $4.15 / $4.60
Latte $3.60 / $4.15 / $4.60

MAP REF. **79**

COFFEE 4.00 / 5	OVERALL 4.00 / 5

Perk Kafé

162 East 37th Street, Manhattan, NY 10016 | **Murray Hill**

Photo courtesy of the venue

The sedate precincts of Murray Hill are probably not the first place you'd think of as the location for a seriously distinguished, extremely laid-back coffee destination. But that's what you get in Perk Kafé. It's not a big place, and can get crowded, but it's worth a visit for the quality of the coffee alone. Beans from Stumptown get the royal treatment, including various non-espresso alternatives if you're a single-origin lover. Latte art is exemplary, and the welcome is friendly. A great place in an unexpected area.

(212) 686-7375
perkkafe.com
Subway 4, 6 (33rd St)

MON–SAT.	7:00am - 7:00pm
SUN.	8:00am - 7:00pm

First opened 2013
Roaster Stumptown Coffee Roasters and guests
Machine La Marzocco, 2 groups
Grinder Mazzer Luigi Super Jolly, Mazzer Luigi Kony

Espresso	$2.95
Cappuccino	$3.95
Latte	$4.25

MAP REF. **80**

COFFEE 4.25 / 5

OVERALL 4.25 / 5 ★★★★⯨

Pushcart Coffee

362 2nd Avenue, Manhattan, NY 10010 | **Gramercy**

This branch of Pushcart likes to think that it places itself at the heart of its local community. While claims like this are common enough, Pushcart pursues the idea with singular devotion. Pictures from the local elementary school are commonplace, and there's a "community board" for flyers and a well-scribbled whiteboard. The airy corner room is equally welcoming to solitary workers and groups of all ages and sizes, and the coffee - bought directly from origin - is expertly made, with great latte art included. A wonderful place indeed.

(917) 224-0761
www.pushcartcoffee.com
Subway L (3rd Ave)

MON-SUN.   7:00am - 7:00pm

First opened 2012
Roaster Pushcart Coffee
Machine La Marzocco, 2 groups
Grinder Mazzer Luigi

Espresso	$3.25
Cappuccino	$4.00
Latte	$4.00 /$4.50 / $5.00

Sister locations Chelsea / Williamsburg

MAP REF. **81**

COFFEE 4.25 / 5		OVERALL 4.25 / 5	

Ramini Espresso Bar

265 West 37th Street, Manhattan, NY 10018 | **Midtown West**

Ramini is a key player in major-league coffee. Its pretty interior has some quirky features and you can always expect an exceptionally warm welcome from coffee-obsessed baristas. The tasty baked goods, are mostly made on the premises and they also offer a superior selection of teas and fresh-squeezed juices. Liquids from the two-group La Marzocco are common, but if you want a real change, go for a cup from the towering 'Kyoto' drip apparatus, the world's slowest drip machine. An unexpected and really delightful find in Midtown.

(347) 907-0343
www.ramininyc.com
Subway A, C, E (34th St - Penn Station)

MON-FRI.   7:00am - 5:30pm
SAT.   9:00am - 1:00pm
SUN.   Closed

First opened 2012
Roaster 49th Parallel Roasters, Vassilaros & Sons
Machine La Marzocco GB5, 2 groups
Grinder Mazzer Luigi Robur

Espresso	$2.75
Cappuccino	$4.00 / $5.75
Latte	$4.00 / $5.75

MAP REF. **82**

COFFEE 4.25 / 5		OVERALL 4.00 / 5	

REX

864 10th Avenue, Manhattan, NY 10039 | **Hell's Kitchen**

REX does its name proud, as this shop is one of the kings. It's got wonderfully prepared coffees from Counter Culture and features a slow bar with seasonal single origins that the staff will happily discuss with you. They also run an astonishingly impressive kitchen, preparing surprises such as house-cured gravlax for fresh sandwiches and impossibly delicious baked goods; the flourless chocolate brownies are one to try. It's a welcome coffee oasis in Hell's Kitchen and though small, it's got two comfy, communal tables and enough charm to make it a cozy, inviting space to visit for a refuel.

(212) 757-0580
www.rexcoffeenyc.com
Subway A, B, C, D (59th St - Columbus Circle)

MON–FRI.	7:00am – 7:00pm
SAT–SUN.	7:00am – 6:00pm

First opened 2013
Roaster Counter Culture Coffee
Machine La Marzocco Linea, 2 groups
Grinder Mazzer Luigi Robur, Mahlkönig EK 43

Espresso	$3.00
Cappuccino	$3.75
Latte	$4.00

MAP REF. 83

COFFEE 4.25 / 5

OVERALL 4.25 / 5 ★★★★

Simon Sips

1185 Avenue of the Americas, Manhattan, NY 10036 | **Midtown West**

Simon Sips is in the business of making good coffee, plain and simple. It embraces a no-nonsense approach to providing exceptional coffee to those who are lucky enough to have found this unexpected shop, settled behind the lobby of a large office building. Head down to this industrious shop from the plaza entrance, open to the public from one of the side streets. The space has a simple, clean interior while their espressos are carefully pulled by attentive baristas. Simon Sips is a welcome little resting place in the bustle of Midtown.

(212) 354-2100
www.simonsips.com
Subway 1,2,3 (42nd Street), 1 (50th St) B,D,F,M (47 - 50th St)

MON-FRI.	7:00am - 5:00pm
SAT-SUN.	Closed

First opened 2008
Roaster Counter Culture Coffee
Machine La Marzocco Linea
Grinder Nuova Simonelli Mythos, Mazzer Luigi

Espresso	$2.75
Cappuccino	$3.75
Latte	$4.25

MAP REF. **84**

COFFEE 4.00 / 5   OVERALL 4.00 / 5

Stumptown Midtown West

Ace Hotel, 18 West 29th Street, Manhattan, NY 10001 | **Midtown West**

Stumptown has expanded considerably in the decade since opening their first New York outpost, but the consistency of the quality here hasn't changed a bit. They offer several types of cold brew including "Nitro". Grab a can as takeaway for later, and order a single origin Chemex pour over. Don't be fooled by the fact that these are not listed on the chalkboard menu; the baristas are verifiable wizards at extracting maximum flavor from the many single-origin bean offerings available.

(855) 711-3385
www.stumptowncoffee.com
Subway N, R (28th St) or 4, 6 (28th St)

MON-FRI.	6:00am - 8:00pm
SAT-SUN.	7:00am - 8:00pm

First opened 2008
Roaster Stumptown Coffee Roasters
Machine La Marzocco Linea, 3 groups
Grinder Mazzer Luigi Robur E

Espresso	$3.25
Cappuccino	$4.00
Latte	$4.00 / $4.50 / $5.00

Sister locations Greenwich Village

MAP REF. **85**

COFFEE 4.50 / 5   OVERALL 4.50 / 5

Taylor St. Baristas

33 East 40th Street, Manhattan, NY 10016 | **Midtown East**

Brand new, Aussie inspired Taylor Street Baristas is an extra ordinary place to spend an afternoon. It's immediately welcoming and upstairs is an inspiring sight for midtowners: tons of space. The constantly-rotating menu features several types of Counter Culture Coffee drip: Classic, Delicate and Wild, each so nuanced. Nothing here feels pretentious thanks to infectiously high-spirited baristas who gladly offer a free taste of each. They're as skilled as they are friendly. The espresso is excellent, as is their flat white made on the gleaming Victoria Arduino Black Eagle.

www.taylor-st.com
Subway 4, 5, 6, 7, S (Grand Central)

MON–FRI. 7:00am – 6:00pm
SAT–SUN. Closed

First opened 2016
Roaster Counter Culture Coffee
Machine Victoria Arduino Black Eagle, 3 groups x2, Victoria Arduino Black Eagle, 2 groups, Marco SP9, 2 groups x2
Grinder Nuova Simonelli Mythos x6, Mahlkönig EK 43 x2

Espresso	$3.50
Cappuccino	$4.25 / $5.00
Latte	$4.25 / $5.00

MAP REF. 86

91

COFFEE 4.75 / 5 🫘🫘🫘🫘🫘

OVERALL 4.50 / 5 ★★★★⯪

Trademark

38 West 36th Street, Manhattan, NY 10018 | **Midtown West**

Midtown Manhattan is full of all kinds of coffee-drinkers, and Trademark seems intent on subtly customizing the experience for each customer. If you're in a hurry and like vanilla lattes, they've got you covered. If you feel like staying a while, they'll make you an excellent, floral single-origin Phoenix pour-over and serve it to you in a beautiful carafe. But you don't want to miss the espresso, extracted on a Mavam matte red espresso machine built into the bar - straight out of the production design of the movie "Her," it's probably the most beautiful espresso machine you've ever seen. Plus there are only about 20 in the world.

(646) 858-2320
www.ingoodcompanyhg.com
Subway B,D,F,M,N,Q,R (34th St, Herald Sq Stn)

MON-SUN. 7:00am - 7:00pm

First opened 2016
Roaster Sweetleaf Coffee Roasters, Lofted Coffee
Machine Custom Mavam
Grinder Mazzer Luigi Kold, Mahlkönig EK 43

Espresso	$3.25
Cappuccino	$4.00
Latte	$4.50

MAP REF. **87**

COFFEE 4.25 / 5	OVERALL 4.25 / 5
🫘🫘🫘🫘🫘	★★★★☆

Zibetto Espresso Bar

501 5th Avenue, Manhattan, NY 10017 | **Midtown East**

Step inside Zibetto and you're not in Manhattan, you're in Milan. This sleek little number, gleaming with marble and tiling, is as authentically Italian as Sophia Loren's smile. The classic Italian short shot of espresso is bracing stuff. There's little seating, in tribute to the Italian view of espresso as something drunk quickly before dashing off. But they don't push you to dash. Though the service is polished and brisk, it's very friendly in a very Italian way. Note: the entrance is around the corner on 42nd Street.

(646) 838-6364
www.zibettoespresso.com
Subway 4, 5, 6 (Grand Central)

Sister locations Midtown

MON-FRI. 7:00am - 7:00pm
SAT. 9:00am - 6:00pm
SUN. 10:00am - 5:00pm

First opened 2014
Roaster Zibetto
Machine La Cimbali M100, 3 groups
Grinder Sanremo

Espresso	$2.50
Cappuccino	$4.25
Latte	$4.50

MAP REF. **88**

COFFEE 4.50 / 5	OVERALL 4.25 / 5
🫘🫘🫘🫘🫘	★★★★☆

**Directly & sustainably
sourced coffee from
all over the world,
locally roasted in the
Hudson Valley.**

Wholesale Inquiries
sales@irvingfarm.com

Classes
education@irvingfarm.com

Everything Else
holler@irvingfarm.com

www.irvingfarm.com

Upper Manhattan

From the Apollo Theatre in Harlem to the world-famous Metropolitan Museum of Art, upper northern Manhattan has a rich and varied cultural heritage. The Upper East Side boasts Museum Row, home to some of the greatest art and history museums in the country, as well as some of the best and most exclusive shopping in New York on Madison Avenue. The Upper West Side has a calmer feel, with the Lincoln Center for the performing Arts and The Museum of Natural History. In between sits the vast Central Park, New York's beloved urban oasis.

Bluestone Lane Upper East Side

TOP 35

2 East 90th Street, Manhattan, NY 10128 | **Upper East Side**

Photo: Ben Hider

Aussie inspired Bluestone Lane has bagged a site that many cafés would kill for: a superb space in a Gothic-style church just across Fifth Avenue from Central Park. Sit in the sandstone interior or grab a table on the sidewalk. The food has a focus on virtue that doesn't sacrifice good flavour, while outstanding house-roasted beans get careful treatment on the La Marzocco. There's a notably warm welcome, and the barista skills extend to outstanding latte art: appropriate when the Guggenheim and Metropolitan are a short walk away and Cooper Hewitt is right across the street.

(646) 869-7812
www.bluestonelaneny.com
Subway 4, 5, 6 (86th St)

Sister locations Greenwich Village / West Village

MON-SUN.   7:30am - 6:00pm

First opened 2015
Roaster Bluestone Lane & Niccolo
Machine La Marzocco Linea, 3 groups
Grinder Nuova Simonelli

Espresso	$2.75
Cappuccino	$4.00
Latte	$4.00

MAP REF. **89**

COFFEE 4.50 / 5	OVERALL 4.50 / 5
🫘🫘🫘🫘🫘	★★★★⯪

Box Kite Upper West Side

128 West 72nd Street, Manhattan, NY 10023 | **Upper West Side**

Photo courtesy of the venue

Upper Manhattan

The lower end of the Upper West Side does not exactly overflow with places for a superior cup, which makes it all the more thrilling that Box Kite chose to open a branch here in 2015. The place is small, with seating for just six people, so the emphasis is inevitably on coffee to take away rather than drink on the premises. But it's an attractive place to sit, and being a WiFi-free zone, it's something of a refuge from the busy world outside.

(212) 574-8203
www.boxkitenyc.com
Subway 1, 2, 3 (72nd St)

Sister locations East Village

MON–SUN. 7:00am – 7:00pm

First opened 2015
Roaster Rotating roasters
Machine Synesso, 2 groups
Grinder Mahlkönig Peak, Mahlkönig EK 40

Espresso	$3.50
Cappuccino	$4.50
Latte	$4.75

MAP REF. **90**

COFFEE 4.25 / 5	OVERALL 4.25 / 5

Café Jax

318 East 84th Street, Manhattan, NY 10028 | **Upper East Side**

Café Jax is a dream of a neighborhood coffee spot. It's a place where all drinks are taken seriously - even as the sense of childlike is preserved in pours such as cold brew ice cream float and lavender lemonade. Stumptown beans make up the house blend, enjoyable in numerous hot and cold forms as you eat a salad, sandwich or baked goods. The long front room is lovely, but the large downstairs seating space and especially the garden, are to be admired.

(212) 510-7084
www.cafejaxnyc.com
Subway 1, 5, 6 (86th St)

MON-SUN.   7:00am - 10:00pm

First opened 2014
Roaster Stumptown Coffee Roasters
Machine La Marzocco Linea, 2 groups
Grinder Mazzer Luigi Major E

Espresso $3.00
Cappuccino $3.75
Latte $4.25

MAP REF. **91**

COFFEE 4.25 / 5   OVERALL 4.00 / 5   ★★★★☆

The Chipped Cup

3610 Broadway, Manhattan, NY 10031 | **Harlem**

This Harlem anchor offers great coffee in a comforting environment. It boasts fresh pastries from Balthazar and toasted bagel sandwiches if you're really peckish to go along with well-drawn shots of Counter Culture espresso. The space is fitted out with lots of tables for all the computer-clacking workers, and there's also a sweet backyard if you're feeling like a breath of fresh air instead.

(212) 368-8881
www.chippedcupcoffee.com
Subway 1 (145 St)

MON-FRI.   7:00am - 8:00pm
SAT-SUN.   8:00am - 8:00pm

First opened 2012
Roaster Counter Culture Coffee
Machine La Marzocco GB5
Grinder Mazzer Luigi Robur E

Espresso $2.75
Cappuccino $3.75
Latte $4.25

MAP REF. **92**

COFFEE 4.00 / 5   OVERALL 4.00 / 5   ★★★★☆

Double Dutch Espresso

2194 Frederick Douglass Boulevard, Manhattan, NY 10026 | **Harlem**

This busy Harlem shop offers a delightful atmosphere for an afternoon coffee respite. Double Dutch serve locally baked treats, make fresh home-made sandwiches and prepare great coffee to charge you through the last few pages of that book you're just aching to finish. There is plenty of seating in a winsome atmosphere, with antique accents that make it feel warm and inviting. They keep two espressos on bar at a time, a blend and a rotating single origin, so be sure to ask what's available.

(646) 429-8834
www.doubledutchespresso.com
Subway A, B, C (Cathedral Pkwy - 110th St)

MON-FRI.	7:00am - 8:00pm
SAT-SUN.	8:00am - 8:00pm

First opened 2013
Roaster Counter Culture Coffee
Machine La Marzocco GB5
Grinder Mazzer Luigi

Espresso	$3.50
Cappuccino	$3.75
Latte	$4.25

MAP REF. **93**

Gregorys Coffee

878 Lexington Avenue, Manhattan, NY 10065 | **Upper East Side**

Gregorys must be doing something right. At the time of writing it has 17 branches and all do a steady-to-roaring trade. This one has an enviable location, with Hunter College nearby, and while the college supplied most business in the early days, now it's much more broadly based. WiFi all week is one draw, but the big room (especially in the back), relaxed vibe, and great brewing from the well-trained team is surely more important. Milky drinks are excellent, and so are single-origin coffees from the drip brewers.

(917) 388-3850
www.gregoryscoffee.com
Subway F (Lexington Ave / 63rd St)

Sister locations Multiple locations

MON-FRI.	6:00am - 8:00pm
SAT.	7:00am - 7:00pm
SUN.	9:00am - 5:00pm

First opened 2015
Roaster Gregorys Coffee
Machine La Marzocco Linea, 3 groups
Grinder Mazzer Luigi Major E,
Mazzer Luigi Kold

Espresso	$3.00
Cappuccino	$4.00
Latte	$4.00

MAP REF. **94**

COFFEE
4.25 / 5

OVERALL
4.25 / 5 ★★★★⯪

Joe Coffee

1045 Lexington Avenue, Manhattan, NY 10021 | **Upper East Side**

Joe has seen new competition arrive since it landed on the Upper East Side in 2011, but it remains a hot favorite with locals. The look is more downtown than uptown, with bare brick and some out-there lampshades. And you'll be lucky to find a seat: there are just a few, in the window and at a communal table. All the hallmark Joe qualities are here in the cup, from great beans (blends or single-origin) through to expert brewing and dazzling latte art.

(212) 988-2500
www.joenewyork.com
Subway 4, 5, 6 (77th St)

Sister locations Joe Pro Shop + HQ and multiple locations

MON-SAT.	7:00am - 8:00pm
SUN.	8:00am - 8:00pm

First opened 2011
Roaster Joe Coffee Roasting
Machine La Marzocco GB5, 2 groups
Grinder Nuova Simonelli Mythos

Espresso	$3.00
Cappuccino	$4.00 / $4.50
Latte	$4.00 / $4.50

MAP REF. **95**

COFFEE 4.50 / 5 🖊🖊🖊🖊🖊   OVERALL 4.25 / 5 ★★★★★

Kuro Kuma Espresso & Coffee

121 La Salle Street, Manhattan, NY 10027 | **Harlem**

Part of Kuro Kuma's success arises from location: this part of Morningside Heights isn't packed with good coffee purveyors. But Kuro Kuma would be smashing it anywhere, however stiff the competition, because this tiny place (seating for six or so) is sensationally good. The coffee is made from Counter Culture beans by highly skilled baristas who take equal care with every type of drink. Even iced coffee, so often a pallid potion, turns to magic here. No wonder Columbia students (and just about everyone else) lines up to buy.

(347) 577-3177
Subway 1 (125th St)

| MON-SAT. | 7:00am - 7:30pm |
| SUN. | 8:00am - 7:30pm |

First opened 2012
Roaster Counter Culture Coffee
Machine La Marzocco GB5
Grinder Mazzer Luigi

Espresso	$2.75
Cappuccino	$4.00
Latte	$4.00

MAP REF. **96**

COFFEE 4.25 / 5   **OVERALL** 4.25 / 5 ★★★★½

The Monkey Cup

1730 Amsterdam Avenue, Manhattan, NY 10031 | **Upper Manhattan**

Laura Leonardi, the Argentinian-born owner of Monkey Cup, trained as a dentist but has now drilled deep into the essence of coffee culture. Her diminutive drop is one of the best places in Harlem for superior cups, either espresso-based or brewed - including the slow-drip cold-brew Kyoto method. The espresso beans change every three months ("We like the variables") and pour-overs are single-origin. This is a warm, friendly place where people love to talk to each other. If you want to guarantee a smile on your face, order a "Monkeyccino."

(646) 665-3906
Subway A, B, C, D (145th St)

MON-FRI.	7:00am - 9:00pm
SAT.	8:00am - 8:00pm
SUN.	8:00am - 6:00pm

First opened 2015
Roaster Irving Farm Coffee Roasters
Machine La Marzocco Linea, 3 groups
Grinder Mahlkönig K 30

Espresso	$2.50
Cappuccino	$3.25
Latte	$3.25

MAP REF. **97**

COFFEE 4.25 / 5   **OVERALL** 4.25 / 5 ★★★★½

Moss Café

3260 Johnson Avenue, The Bronx, NY 10463 | **Kingsbridge**

Photo courtesy o' the venue

They're all about things local and fresh at Moss Café, as the shop bustles with neighbors and families who come in to enjoy the healthy food and charming environment. One of the first third wave coffee shops to come to the Bronx, Moss Cafe shares Stumptown beans with the neighbors alongside house made baked goods and menu of seasonal fare that all happens to be Kosher too. You'll even find gluten free and dairy-free items, so it's pretty easy to find something delicious and wholesome to go along with your lovely latte.

(347) 275-5000
www.mosscafeny.com
Subway 1 (238th St)

MON–THU.	7:00am - 9:00pm
FRI.	7:00am - 4:00pm
SAT.	Closed
SUN.	8:00am - 9:00pm

First opened 2015
Roaster Stumptown Coffee Roasters
Machine La Marzocco GB5, 2 groups
Grinder Mazzer Luigi Kony E, Mazzer Luigi Super Jolly E

Espresso	$2.50
Cappuccino	$3.75
Latte	$4.00

MAP REF. **98**

COFFEE 4.00 / 5

OVERALL 4.00 / 5 ★★★★☆

102

Oslo Coffee Roasters Upper East Side

422 East 75th Street, Manhattan, NY 10021 | **Upper East Side**

Oslo's Yorkville location is a tiny neighborhood caffeinery with a big heart. The baristas welcome local customers as if they were old friends - which many of them appear to be. The real star here is the old, lovingly maintained authentic San Marco espresso machine - a manual job complete with gleaming levers. Baristas pull great shots of Oslo's creamy espresso blend using those levers, and watching them at work is an all-too-rare pleasure.

(718) 782-0332
www.oslocoffee.com
Subway 4, 6 (77th St)

Sister locations Williamsburg

MON-FRI.	7:00am - 7:00pm
SAT-SUN.	8:00am - 7:00pm
	(6:00pm in winter)

First opened 2011
Roaster Oslo Coffee Roasters
Machine San Marco, 3 groups
Grinder Mazzer Luigi Robur

Espresso	$3.00
Cappuccino	$3.75
Latte	$3.75

MAP REF. **99**

COFFEE 4.25 / 5   OVERALL 4.25 / 5 ★★★★⯪

Petite Shell

1269 Lexington Avenue, Manhattan, NY 10028 | **Upper East Side**

Petite Shell marries serious coffee with a perfect companion - freshly baked rugelach. They offer a variety of inventive flavors, like pear blue cheese and chocolate Nutella cream, that pair perfectly with their coffees. They offer three different kinds of iced coffee (Kyoto, ice-brewed and cold brewed) as well as a pour-over bar. The space is bright and gleaming, with sunlight that soaks the space in a warm, inviting glow.

(212) 828-2233
Subway 4, 5, 6 (86th St)

MON-FRI.	7:00am - 8:00pm
SAT.	7:00am - 10:00pm
SUN.	7:00am - 8:00pm

First opened 2015
Roaster 40 Weight
Machine La Marzocco Linea
Grinder Nuova Simonelli

Espresso	$2.50
Cappuccino	$3.50
Latte	$4.00

MAP REF. **100**

COFFEE 4.25 / 5   OVERALL 4.25 / 5 ★★★★⯪

Plowshares

2730 Broadway, Manhattan, NY 10025 | **Upper West Side**

Plowshares opened this spot quietly, but word of mouth travels quickly in this town, and their wonderfully prepared coffees are making waves among the caffeinated elite. They roast their own coffees and serve them with care at this 11-seat shop. They only have one blend here, while all the others are single origin varieties from across the coffee-producing world. They offer at least two batch-brewed coffees at a time, a pour-over bar, and both a regular and nitrogen-infused cold brew that's extra rich and caffeinated.

(212) 222-0285
www.plowsharescoffee.com
Subway 1 (103rd St)

MON-FRI.	7:00am - 7:00pm
SAT-SUN.	8:00am - 7:00pm

First opened 2014
Roaster Plowshares Coffee Roasters
Machine Slayer, 2 groups
Grinder Mahlkönig K30, Mahlkönig EK 43

Espresso	$2.75
Cappuccino	$4.00
Latte	$4.50

MAP REF. **101**

COFFEE 4.25 / 5

OVERALL 4.25 / 5 ★★★★⯪

Uptown Roasters

135 East 110th Street, Manhattan, NY 10029 | **East Harlem**

East Harlem has relatively few independent artisanal coffee places, so the arrival of Uptown was a boon for locals. And both long-time residents and newer 'yuppie' arrivals have taken to the place. It's small and quiet, with simple brick-and-wood décor that provides a perfect hangout and a showcase for beans from the roastery in the South Bronx. The owners have a Peruvian background, so there's an emphasis on South American beans. Pour-over is the best way to appreciate single-origin, but espresso-based drinks are made carefully.

(646) 918-6600
www.uptownroasters.com
Subway 6 (110th St)

MON-FRI.	6:00am - 6:00pm
SAT-SUN.	7:30am - 6:00pm

First opened 2015
Roaster Uptown Roasters
Machine Rancilio Epoca, 2 groups
Grinder Mahlkönig Guatemala, Mazzer Luigi Super Jolly

Espresso	$2.50
Cappuccino	$3.25
Latte	$4.00

MAP REF. **102**

COFFEE 4.25 / 5

OVERALL 4.25 / 5 ★★★★⯪

Park Slope
& Surrounding

The largely residential neighborhoods of Park Slope, Kensington, Ditmas Park, Crown Heights and Prospect Gardens make up this area of Brooklyn. Kensington and Ditmas Park still retain many examples of beautiful Victorian architecture, while Prospect Heights is known for its rich cultural history. The Brooklyn Botanical Gardens, The Brooklyn Museum and The Pratt Institute all be found there. Park Slope itself, with its picturesque tree-lined streets, historic brownstones, popular restaurants and shops, is a great neighborhood to explore.

BROOKLYN PUBLIC LIBRARY

Breukelen Coffee House

764a Franklin Avenue, Brooklyn, NY 11238 | **Prospect Heights**

Photo courtesy of the venue

Breukelen Coffee House has been a staple venue in Crown Heights since it first opened in 2009, and after spending some time inside, it's easy to see why. The relaxed atmosphere is the perfect spot for everyone, from Crown Heights hipsters to white collar Wall Street. The espresso is strong, the pastries are sweet, and the baristas treat every customer as if they are a regular. Expertly brewed Stumptown beans are served with enthusiasm. For food, pastries are sold alongside a seasonal menu of light fare prepared with locally sourced ingredients.

(718) 789-7070
www.breukelencoffeehouse.com
Subway 2, 3, 4, 5 (Franklin Ave)

| MON-FRI. | 7:00am – 8:00pm |
| SAT-SUN. | 8:00am – 8:00pm |

First opened 2009
Roaster Stumptown Coffee Roasters
Machine La Marzocco, 2 groups
Grinder Mazzer Luigi Major

Espresso	$2.30
Cappuccino	$3.75
Latte	$4.00

MAP REF. 103

COFFEE 4.00 / 5   OVERALL 4.00 / 5 ★★★★☆

Café Regular du Nord

158a Berkeley Place, Brooklyn, NY 11217 | **Park Slope**

Photo courtesy of the venue

Good things come in small packages. Café Regular du Nord is a beautiful café with vintage vibes, from the funky painting on the wall to the crystal chandelier. The espresso-based beverages are great, but the best quality of this café is its versatile menu, where there is something for adults and kids alike. Not a coffee drinker, or bringing the kids with you? No need to worry, delicious Jacques Torres hot chocolate is served here. Teachers and students, be sure to take advantage of the discounts offered.

(718) 783-0673
www.caferegular.com
Subway B, Q (7th Avenue) or 2, 3, 4 (Grand Army Plaza)

Sister locations Park Slope

MON–SUN.   7:00am - 7:00pm

First opened 2009
Roaster La Colombe Torrefaction Coffee Roasters
Machine La Marzocco FB80, 2 groups
Grinder Mazzer Luigi, Super Jolly E

Espresso	$3.00
Cappuccino	$4.00
Latte	$4.00

MAP REF. **104**

COFFEE 4.00 / 5	OVERALL 4.00 / 5

Gorilla Coffee

472 Bergen Street, Brooklyn, NY 11217 | **Park Slope**

Gorilla's Park Slope branch, its second in Brooklyn, is a big, modern, functionally decorated place with very fifties-looking tables. Somehow none of that makes it feel institutional, because this is a comfortable place to sit and hang out. Gorilla has been roasting in Brooklyn since 2002 and their full variety is shown best in the Chemex or pour-over, but espresso-based drinks are made to the same high standards. Baked goods are very popular; but don't be surprised if the selection's shrunk if you get there later in the day.

www.gorillacoffee.com
Subway 2, 3, 4, 5, N, Q, R, W, M (Atlantic Ave / Pacific St)

MON–SAT.	7:00am – 9:00pm
SUN.	8:00am – 9:00pm

First opened 2014
Roaster Gorilla Coffee
Machine La Marzocco Strada, 3 groups
Grinder Mazzer Luigi Robur

Espresso	$2.50
Cappuccino	$3.50
Latte	$3.50

MAP REF. **105**

COFFEE 4.25 / 5

OVERALL 4.25 / 5 ★★★★⯪

Hungry Ghost

253 Flatbush Avenue, Brooklyn, NY 11217 | **Prospect Heights**

Photo courtesy of the venue

Sleek is the first word that comes to mind upon entering the Hungry Ghost Coffee Bar & Café. With its cool gray undertones and comfortable seating, it is the perfect spot to relax with a cold brew and one of their much sought after scones. Conversation and community is encouraged within the space, as laptop use is restricted to a select area. This emphasis on community, combined with the quality of product, makes Hungry Ghost a Prospect Heights destination for everyone from coffee connoisseurs to creative collaborators.

(718) 483-8666
www.hungryghostbrooklyn.com
Subway 2, 3, 4 (Bergen St)

Sister locations Fort Greene / Greenwich Village / Prospect Heights

MON-SUN. 6:30am - 9:00pm

First opened 2012
Roaster Stumptown Coffee Roasters
Machine La Marzocco GB5
Grinder Mazzer Luigi Robur

Espresso	$2.75
Cappuccino	$3.25
Latte	$4.00

MAP REF. 106

COFFEE 4.25 / 5	OVERALL 4.25 / 5

Little Zelda

728 Franklin Avenue, Brooklyn, NY 11238 | **Crown Heights**

Little Zelda is the quintessential neighborhood spot, a charming little space where coffee isn't just a beverage but something that brings people together. You'll find local writers and readers getting literary while sipping lattes at this delightfully vintage café with well-used and ever lovely Toby's Estate coffees. There's a community board where people looking for roommates or apartments may post to find a match. This cozy shop and its cheery staff make Little Zelda a lovely little home away from home.

(646) 320-7347
Subway S (Park Pl)

MON-FRI.	7:00am – 6:00pm
SAT-SUN.	8:00am – 6:00pm

First opened 2012
Roaster Toby's Estate Coffee
Machine La Marzocco Linea, 2 groups
Grinder Mazzer Luigi Major

Espresso	$2.50
Cappuccino	$3.50
Latte	$4.00

MAP REF. 107

COFFEE 4.00 / 5 🖊🖊🖊🖊🖊 **OVERALL** 4.00 / 5 ★★★★☆

Manhattanville Coffee

167 Rogers Avenue, Brooklyn, NY 11216 | **Crown Heights**

Manhattanville is a welcome sight on one of those long Crown Heights blocks that offer little in the way of refreshment. Order from the counter, staffed by friendly young people, then settle down with your friends or your laptop. There are also board games on hand if you need other entertainment, and families are particularly welcome. The walls are an attractive dark gray, the coffee is expertly made using Intelligentsia beans, and the food is fully kosher. Manhattanville is an unusual but delightful coffee spot.

(646) 781-9900
www.manhattanvillecoffee.com
Subway 2, 3, 4 (Nostrand Ave)

MON-FRI.	6:30am – 8:00pm
SAT-SUN.	7:30am – 8:00pm

First opened 2015
Roaster Intelligentsia Coffee
Machine La Marzocco GB5, 2 groups
Grinder Mahlkönig EK 43

Espresso	$2.50
Cappuccino	$3.50
Latte	$4.00

Sister locations Harlem   MAP REF. 108

COFFEE 4.00 / 5 🖊🖊🖊🖊🖊 **OVERALL** 4.25 / 5 ★★★★☆

Milk Bar

620 Vanderbilt Avenue, Brooklyn, NY 11238 | **Prospect Heights**

Tiny, light-filled Milk Bar is run like a restaurant - a waiter acts as host, seating your party when you arrive. In other hands, this type of set-up could feel highly-strung, but the staff are so pleasant that having the attention of a waiter is a relaxed affair. Located in Prospect Heights, it's a quiet neighborhood shop, but is also good enough to go out of your way for. You can't go wrong with the drinks here - Counter Culture provides the beans - but honor the shop's Australian roots and go with the excellent, strong flat white.

(718) 230-0844
www.milkbarbrooklyn.com
Subway 2, 3, 4 (Grand Army Plaza) or B, Q (7th Ave)

MON-FRI.	7:30am - 5:00pm
SAT-SUN.	8:00am - 6:00pm

First opened 2009
Roaster Counter Culture Coffee
Machine La Marzocco Linea, 2 groups
Grinder Mazzer Luigi

Espresso	$3.50
Cappuccino	$4.00
Latte	$4.50

MAP REF. 109

COFFEE 4.25 / 5

OVERALL 4.25 / 5

Qathra

1112 Cortelyou Road, Brooklyn, NY 11218 | **Ditmas Park**

This Ditmas Park neighborhood shop has developed quite a following, and when you taste the coffee it's easy to see why. Despite its unassuming hand-painted decor (think 1990s Portland) Qathra is deadly serious about its coffee. Don't add milk to the excellent, robust Hario pour-overs. If you do happen to be in the mood for something milky, indulge in a frothy, sweet latte. Snag a spot in the delightful backyard and start wondering why you haven't already moved to Brooklyn.

(347) 305-3250
www.qathracafe.com
Subway Q (Cortelyou Rd)

MON-SUN. 7:00am - 9:00pm

First opened 2010
Roaster Café Integral
Machine La Marzocco Strada MP
Grinder Mazzer Luigi

Espresso $2.50
Cappuccino $3.50
Latte $4.00

MAP REF. 110

| COFFEE 4.25 / 5 | 🫘🫘🫘🫘◗ | OVERALL 4.25 / 5 | ★★★★⯪ |

Roots Cafe

639a Fifth Avenue, Brooklyn, NY 11215 | **Park Slope**

In many ways, walking into Roots Café feels like walking into someone's home. Along the walls hang quirky paintings, musical instruments, and bookshelves filled with the classics. The 'hominess' is not merely aesthetic; it is a quality that extends to the service. Walk through to the counter in the back and interact with the engaging baristas who serve excellent espresso-based beverages alongside a variety of breakfast and lunch sandwiches. If you're craving something sweet, be sure to try the salted caramel latte or peppermint mocha.

(615) 419-7877
www.rootsbrooklyn.com
Subway D, N, R (Prospect Ave)

MON-FRI. 6:30am - 6:00pm
SAT-SUN. 8:00am - 6:00pm

First opened 2008
Roaster Forty Weight Coffee Roasters
Machine La Marzocco Linea
Grinder La Marzocco

Espresso $2.50
Cappuccino $3.50
Latte $4.00

MAP REF. 111

| COFFEE 4.25 / 5 | 🫘🫘🫘🫘◗ | OVERALL 4.00 / 5 | ★★★★☆ |

Stonefruit Espresso + Kitchen

1058 Bedford Avenue, Brooklyn, NY 11205 | **Bed-Stuy**

A major spot for Bed-Stuy, Stonefruit is a little slice of Los Angeles, in the best sense possible. It's a coffee shop, it's a florist, it's a candle and used-book shop, it's a restaurant that serves wine. Comfortable rope-swing chairs hang from the ceiling in this beautifully designed, light-filled space. The baristas are perfectionists at handling milk. The single-origin pour-overs are delicious, but the flat white is even better. The matcha latte is just as good; it's hard to choose what to drink here because they get everything right.

(718) 230-4147
www.stonefruitespresso.com
Subway G (Classon Ave)

MON–FRI.   7:30am – 6:00pm
SAT–SUN.   8:30am – 6:00pm

First opened 2015
Roaster Counter Culture Coffee
Machine La Marzocco GB5, 2 groups
Grinder Nuova Simonelli Mythos Clima Pro

Espresso $3.00
Cappuccino $3.75
Latte $4.25

MAP REF. 112

COFFEE 4.50 / 5   🫘🫘🫘🫘🫘

OVERALL 4.50 / 5   ★★★★⯪

Tygershark

581 Vanderbilt Avenue, Brooklyn, NY 11238 | **Prospect Heights**

Photo courtesy of the venue

Tygershark proves once and for all that a chilled barista can also be a perfectionist barista. First and foremost an ultra-hip (and excellent) Korean restaurant and bar, with a coffee bar/surfshop in the front - yes, you can buy a surfboard should the urge strike you. The beautiful, Sydney-esque space features a lovely backyard. The atmosphere couldn't be more laid-back, and the espresso drinks couldn't be better.

(718) 576-6233
www.tygershark.nyc
Subway A,C (Clinton - Washington Aves)

MON.	Closed
TUE-FRI.	8:30am - 4:00pm
SAT-SUN.	9:00am - 5:30pm
	(5:30pm - 11:00pm for dinner)

First opened 2015
Roaster Concave
Machine La Marzocco Linea, 2 groups
Grinder Mazzer Luigi Kony, Mahlkönig EK 43

Espresso	$3.00
Cappuccino	$4.00
Latte	$4.25

MAP REF. 113

COFFEE 4.25 / 5   **OVERALL** 4.25 / 5 ★★★★☆

DIGITAL CUPS

Introducing Detpak's revolutionary cup capability... high quality photographic print with optional high-build varnish. With no plate charges and low run quantities starting at 5,000 cups this is the new reality!

WWW.DETPAK.COM

Tel: +1-253-380-5091
Email: cups@detpak.com

Downtown Brooklyn

With The Brooklyn Academy of Music in Fort Greene, the beautiful and historic Promenade along the water in Brooklyn Heights and all the fashionable shops and restaurants in Carroll Gardens and Cobble Hill, it's easy to wander a day away in Downtown Brooklyn. These largely residential areas are filled with beautiful tree-lined streets and quiet parks, and are known for being home to many of New York's greatest artists, writers and musicians.

Brewklyn Grind

557 Myrtle Avenue, Brooklyn, NY 11205 | **Clinton Hill**

Photo courtesy of the venue

In 2006, the three Farrelly brothers from Bay Ridge Brooklyn - an engineer, a banker and a high school drop-out - opened a roastery in Red Hook. Before long, they were serving high profile clients like Facebook, and opening this quiet, unassuming neighborhood shop. An impressive 40% of their beans come from farmers they have a direct relationship with. Go for a single origin pour over, or the ultra-strong but somehow still sweet and silky cold brew. Brewklyn Grind features a lovely backyard which fills up with students from the nearby Pratt Institute.

(347) 452-8866
www.bkgcoffee.com
Subway G (Classon Avenue)

MON-SUN. 8:00am - 6:00pm

First opened 2014
Roaster Brewklyn Grind Coffee Roasters
Machine Faema E61
Grinder Mazzer Luigi

Espresso	$2.75
Cappuccino	$3.75
Latte	$4.50

MAP REF. 114

COFFEE 4.25 / 5

OVERALL 4.25 / 5

121

Brooklyn Roasting Company Dumbo

25 Jay Street, Brooklyn, NY 11201 | **Dumbo**

Brooklyn's flagship Navy Yard branch is a big, bustling operation that packs in customers of just about every age. Hipsters abound, but so do toddlers. This is one thing that makes the place so lively. Brooklyn Roasting Company offers a large and varied food menu and a good selection of non-caffeinated drinks such as fresh juices, and smoothies. But the coffee is the real star here, whether well-made milky drinks or daily brewed coffees (a changing selection) from excellent single-origin beans. Sit back and watch live roasting in operation at one end of this enormous café.

(718) 514-2874
www.brooklynroasting.com
Subway F (York St)

Sister locations Flatiron District / Greenpoint / Navy Yard

MON–SUN. 7:00am - 7:00pm

First opened 2010
Roaster Brooklyn Roasting Company
Machine La Marzocco Linea GB5, 2 groups
Grinder Nuova Simonelli Mythos

Espresso	$2.50
Cappuccino	$3.75
Latte	$4.50

MAP REF. 115

COFFEE 4.50 / 5	OVERALL 4.50 / 5
	★★★★⯪

Nobletree

499 Van Brunt Street, Brooklyn, NY 11231 | **Red Hook**

Photo courtesy of the venue

New to the Red Hook area, this fantastic roastery and café certainly impresses. From the breath-taking location which enjoys beautiful views of the Statue of Liberty and New York Harbor, to the magnificent roastery and tasting room which visitors are encouraged to tour and indulge in the soil-to-sip experience. Nobletree's own beans are grown on their award-winning farms in Brazil and pulled through their impressive ModBar. Nobletree is a must see.

(718) 305-4255
www.nobletreecoffee.com
Subway F, G (Smith - 9 St)

Sister locations Financial District

MON–SUN. 8:00am - 5:00pm

First opened 2016
Roaster Nobletree
Machine ModBar
Grinder Mahlkönig Peak

Espresso	$3.00
Cappuccino	$4.00
Latte	$4.50

MAP REF. 116

COFFEE   PENDING   OVERALL   PENDING

Smith Canteen

343 Smith Street, Brooklyn, NY 11231 | **Carroll Gardens**

Photo courtesy of the venue

Smith Canteen is bright and welcoming, a true gem in Brooklyn's Carroll Park area. It is not surprising for the line to be out the door, but the wait is always worth it. From coffee brewed to perfection, to their variety of organic pastries, the café is committed to serving quality products. Being environmentally conscious is important to the café; they serve Counter Culture beans, a roaster that prides itself on sustainability. Even during peak hours, baristas engage in personalized conversation with customers.

(718) 422-0444
www.smithcanteen.com
Subway F, G (Carroll St)

MON-SUN.   7:00am - 5:00pm

First opened 2011
Roaster Counter Culture Coffee
Machine La Marzocco Linea
Grinder Mazzer Luigi

Espresso	$2.50
Cappuccino	$4.00
Latte	$4.50

COFFEE 4.25 / 5   **OVERALL** 4.25 / 5   ★★★★⯪

124

INSPIRING BEAUTIFUL COFFEE MOMENTS SINCE 1933

illy

For three generations, the Illy family has spent eight decades refining a singular blend of coffee, sustainably sourced from the top 1% of Arabica beans grown worldwide.

Perfected for Italian espresso and enjoyed in your favorite coffee beverage, delight in the beautiful taste of illy.

Discover illy at 2Beans.

live
happilly

2|beans
COFFEE & CHOCOLATE PASSION

100 Park Ave. • 254 Park Ave. S.
461 Amsterdam Ave. • 1000 8th Ave. – Turnstyle

Bushwick & Surrounding

Featuring the Northern part of Brooklyn, Bushwick is fast becoming one of the most sought after neighborhoods. Spilling over from trendy Williamsburg, cafes, restaurants and boutiques are all finding new spots to feature their expanding retail offerings. With neighboring Bedford–Stuyvesant expanding from Bushwick this area now has a lot to be desired.

AP Café

420 Troutman Street, Brooklyn, NY 11237 | **Bushwick**

AP Café is a beautifully minimalist café that lets its fine coffee and food take focus within its vast, white-washed walls. The shop is bright, fresh, and the perfect spot to grab a drink and partake in its extensive menu of food offerings, ranging from quinoa bowls to freshly prepared seasonal juices. The coffee comes from Toby's Estate, and the menu features specialty drinks like Vietnamese iced coffee.

(347) 404-6147
www.apcafenyc.com
Subway L (Jefferson St)

MON–THU.	8:00am – 5:00pm
FRI.	8:00am – 7:00pm
SAT–SUN.	9:00am – 7:00pm

First opened 2013
Roaster Toby's Estate Coffee
Machine Faema E61 Legend
Grinder Bunn

Espresso	$2.50
Cappuccino	$3.75
Latte	$4.00

MAP REF. 118

COFFEE 4.25 / 5   **OVERALL** 4.25 / 5   ★★★★☆

Brunswick

144 Decatur Street, Brooklyn, NY 11233 | **Bed-Stuy**

The Bedford-Stuyvesant location of Brunswick welcomes you with large windows and an impressive geometric interior design. The well-designed space affords both sit-down and to-go services. Its menu features light fare focusing on delicious brunch and lunch items, and Counter Culture beans are perfectly brewed on the La Marzocco. The sit-down service is excellent, food is made to order quickly and served with a smile. Whether you're meeting friends for brunch or looking for a work spot, Brunswick has got you covered.

(347) 404-6832
www.brunswickcafe.com
Subway A, C (Kingston - Throops Avs)

Sister locations Windsor Terrace

MON–FRI.	7:30am – 5:00pm
SAT–SUN.	8:30am – 6:00pm

First opened 2014
Roaster Counter Culture Coffee
Machine La Marzocco Linea, 2 groups
Grinder Mazzer Luigi Robur E

Espresso	$3.00
Cappuccino	$4.00
Latte	$4.50

MAP REF. 119

COFFEE 4.00 / 5   **OVERALL** 4.25 / 5   ★★★★☆

Bunna Cafe

1084 Flushing Avenue, Brooklyn, NY 11237 | **Bushwick**

If you don't speak Amharic you might not even realize that the coffee is a speciality at Bunna Cafe, a delicious, relaxed Ethiopian restaurant (in Amharic Bunna means coffee). There's only one option here: a thick, intensely aromatic hand-poured coffee flavored with cardamom and clove - with sugar or without (we recommend with sugar). If you're able to come on a weekend at 5pm, or select weeknights at 6pm, you get to see and even participate in a traditional Bunna ceremony. Essentially, you get to watch, and more importantly, smell a coffee expert handwash, handroast, and hand-pour the coffee. It's safe to say you'll never in your life have more freshly-roasted coffee than this.

MON-FRI.	12:00pm - 11:00pm
SAT-SUN.	11:00am - 11:00pm

First opened 2016

(347) 295-2227
www.bunnaethiopia.net
Subway L (Jefferson St) or L (Morgan Ave)

MAP REF. **120**

COFFEE 4.00 / 5	OVERALL 4.00 / 5
🫘🫘🫘🫘🫘	★★★★☆

Caffe Vita Bushwick

576 Johnson Avenue, Brooklyn, NY 11237 | **Bushwick**

Right in the still-industrial heart of old Bushwick, Caffe Vita's roaster/café has plenty of seating and a bird's eye view of the roaster in action. The Vita folks buy beans direct from producers, something they championed at an early stage in third-wave coffee history, and they put the product to great use. In addition to expertly-made pour-over and espresso-based drinks, you shouldn't miss out on their sweetened take on nitro-brewed cold brew, as well as their unconventional rolls.

(929) 295-9328
www.caffevita.com
Subway L (Jefferson St)

Sister locations Lower East Side

MON-FRI.	8:00am - 6:00pm
SAT-SUN.	8:00am - 4:00pm

First opened 2015
Roaster Caffe Vita
Machine Kees van der Westen, 3 groups
Grinder Mazzer Luigi Super Jolly

Espresso	$3.25
Cappuccino	$4.65
Latte	$4.65

MAP REF. **121**

COFFEE 4.25 / 5	OVERALL 4.50 / 5
🫘🫘🫘🫘🫘	★★★★⯪

City of Saints Bushwick

299 Meserole Street, Brooklyn, NY 11206 | **Bushwick**

The industrial part of Bushwick is full of warehouses, many of which are being converted into trendy businesses and fancy apartments. Refreshingly, City of Saints still feels very much like a warehouse, with its corrugated metal pull-down door entrance and a beautiful graffiti mural decorating one of its walls. This is where City of Saints roast their beans - in full view, if you're curious to watch - with a few café tables in front. Their excellent coffee bar always has a constantly rotating selection to tempt you, but for an ultimate palate experience, the cold brew is the one to try.

(929) 900-5282
www.cityofsaintscoffee.com
Subway L (Montrose Ave)

MON-FRI. 8:00am - 5:30pm
SAT-SUN. 10:00am - 5:30pm

First opened 2015
Roaster City of Saints Coffee Roaster
Machine Victoria Arduino Black Eagle
Grinder Nuova Simonelli Mythos One

Espresso	$3.00
Cappuccino	$3.75
Latte	$4.00

Sister locations East Village

MAP REF. **122**

COFFEE 4.50 / 5	OVERALL 4.25 / 5

Little Skips

941 Willoughby Avenue, Brooklyn, NY 11211 | **Bushwick**

Photo courtesy of the venue

Little Skips is a total neighborhood haunt, with a clientele of young artists and intellectuals who sit and work for hours. Come join in and sip on a nice espresso while finishing your latest book. Or just sit back and enjoy their quality coffees from Counter Culture in this laid-back shop. Little Skips also offers freshly prepared sandwiches, great vegan treats and cool tunes.

(718) 484-0980
www.littleskips.com
Subway M (Central Ave)

Sister locations Bushwick

MON-FRI.	7:00am - 9:00pm
SAT-SUN.	8:00am - 9:00pm

First opened 2010
Roaster Counter Culture Coffee
Machine La Marzocco Linea
Grinder Mazzer Luigi Robur E

Espresso	$2.75
Cappuccino	$3.75
Latte	$4.00 / $4.50

MAP REF. **123**

COFFEE 4.25 / 5   🫘 🫘 🫘 🫘 🫘

OVERALL 4.00 / 5   ★ ★ ★ ★ ☆

Milk & Pull Bushwick

181 Irving Avenue, Brooklyn, NY 11237 | **Bushwick**

Photo courtesy of the venue

Milk & Pull couldn't be a more unassuming local, nestled in a quiet block in Bushwick with just a few seats outside and a modest frontage. But it's a wonderful place, with a long, narrow, brightly-painted interior and a tempting array of baked goodies to ogle while waiting for your coffee, which is exceptionally well made. Stumptown beans are treated royally on the La Marzocco and there is great latte art even on a macchiato. Milk & Pull has a solid core of regulars; you'll see why they keep on coming back.

(347) 627-8511
www.milkandpull.com
Subway L (DeKalb Ave)

Sister locations Ridgewood

MON-FRI.	7:00am - 6:00pm
SAT.	8:00am - 6:00pm
SUN.	8:00am - 5:00pm

First opened 2013
Roaster Stumptown Coffee Roasters
Machine La Marzocco Linea, 2 groups
Grinder Mazzer Luigi Robur E

Espresso	$3.00
Cappuccino	$3.50
Latte	$4.00

MAP REF. **124**

COFFEE 4.25 / 5

OVERALL 4.25 / 5 ★★★★⯪

Milk & Pull Ridgewood

778 Seneca Avenue, Queens, NY 11385 | **Ridgewood**

Photo courtesy of the venue

This Ridgewood outpost of Milk & Pull brings well-made coffee to this burgeoning neighborhood. The menu features coffee from Portland star roaster Stumptown with espressos and cold brew, a standard for serious cafés today. They prepare fresh sandwiches and bagels and offer a nice variety of local baked goods. Exposed brick and natural wood make up the bright, airy place that features large tables spread leisurely apart, allowing for plenty of space to sit and relax.

(718) 821-1155
www.milkandpull.com
Subway M (Seneca Ave)

Sister locations Bushwick

MON-FRI.	7:00am - 7:00pm
SAT.	8:00am - 7:00pm
SUN.	8:00am - 6:00pm

First opened 2015
Roaster Stumptown Coffee Roasters
Machine La Marzocco GB5
Grinder Mazzer Luigi Super Jolly

Espresso	$3.00
Cappuccino	$3.50
Latte	$4.00

MAP REF. **125**

COFFEE
4.25 / 5

OVERALL
4.00 / 5 ★★★★☆

132

Strangeways

87 St Nicholas Avenue, Brooklyn, NY 11237 | **Bushwick**

Photo: Katharina Poblotzki

This cool Bushwick spot spins records and pulls shots with skill and swagger. They don't do blends here (or decaf!), instead offering a variety of single origins from roasters like Lofted Coffee and Four Barrel. The menu is updated often, structured like a family tree so you can follow the seasonal coffees and how they're prepared, right back to their roots. The shop has an Americana-desert feel; reclaimed wood and succulents punctuate the small shop while old school beats fill the space, playing from their library of cassettes and records.

Subway L (Jefferson St)

| MON-FRI. | 7:00am – 5:00pm |
| SAT-SUN. | 8:00am – 5:00pm |

First opened 2013
Roaster Four Barrel, Lofted Coffee and guests
Machine La Marzocco Linea, 3 groups
Grinder Mazzer Luigi Robur

Espresso	$3.50
Cappuccino	$4.50
Latte	$5.00

MAP REF. 126

COFFEE 4.25 / 5

OVERALL 4.25 / 5 ★★★★☆

Supercrown Coffee Roasters

8 Wilson Avenue, Brooklyn, NY 11237 | **Bushwick**

Darleen Scherer founded Gorilla Coffee before setting up Supercrown, and her experience in high-end quality shows in every aspect of this impressive café/roastery in light-industrial Bushwick. It used to be an automotive glass shop, and you can imagine SUVs in the space where their vintage Probat now turns out fragrant beans behind a big window - a spectator sport for those drinking on the premises. Pour-over and espresso-based drinks are equally good, but you owe it to yourself to try their coffee lemonade - an exquisite drink by any measure.

(347) 295-3161
www.supercrown.coffee
Subway L (Morgan Ave)

MON-SUN. 7:00am - 7:00pm

First opened 2016
Roaster Supercrown Coffee Roaster
Machine La Marzocco Strada, 3 groups
Grinder Nuova Simonelli Mythos

Espresso	$3.00
Cappuccino	$4.00
Latte	$4.25 / $4.50

MAP REF. **127**

COFFEE 4.75 / 5	🫘🫘🫘🫘🫘	OVERALL 4.50 / 5	★★★★⯪

Variety Coffee Roasters Bushwick

146 Wyckoff Avenue, Brooklyn, NY 11237 | **Bushwick**

Any place where you can play Ms Pac Man on a real arcade table has got to be legendary, and this big Variety flagship boasts exactly that. But it's not all fun and games here, as plenty of people sit and work. The décor is dominated by white paint, dark wood and exposed brick. The coffee offering is Variety's usual high-class stuff, brewed by experts using beans roasted at the back of the room. Service is swift and friendly, and you can get plenty of sound advice about what to drink.

(718) 497-2326
www.varietycoffeeroasters.com
Subway L (DeKalb Ave)

Sister locations Greenpoint / Williamsburg

MON-SUN. 7:00am - 9:00pm

First opened 2014
Roaster Variety Coffee Roasters
Machine La Marzocco Linea, 3 groups
Grinder Mazzer Luigi Robur E

Espresso	$2.50
Cappuccino	$3.50
Latte	$4.00

MAP REF. 128

COFFEE 4.75 / 5	OVERALL 4.50 / 5

Walter's Coffee Roastery

65 Irving Avenue, Brooklyn, NY 11237 | **Bushwick**

Photo courtesy of the venue

Fresh to the New York coffee scene, Walter's Coffee was founded in Istanbul and is now expanding with this Bushwick store and a new venue in Dubai. In the words of Walter's, "we respect coffee and its chemistry. We have coffee down to a science." Owner Deniz has over 10 years of experience in the industry and has used his knowledge to create something amazing. From their signature yellow suits to their magnificent coffee, Walter's Coffee is one to watch.

(646) 642-3267
www.walterscoffeeroastery.com
Subway L (Jefferson St)

MON-THU.	7:00am - 10:00pm
FRI-SAT.	7:00am - 12:00am
SUN.	9:00am - 10:00pm

First opened 2016
Roaster Walter's Coffee Roasters
Machine Mavam UCME, 2 groups
Grinder Mahlkönig K30

Espresso	$3.00
Cappuccino	$3.75
Latte	$4.25

MAP REF. **129**

COFFEE PENDING   OVERALL PENDING

◊ TOP 35

Williamsburg

Williamsburg is a popular, trendy neighborhood with a lively, youthful feel. This area is a mecca for foodies, featuring lots of coffee roasteries housed in its converted warehouses, the Smorgasburg food market on the waterfront in the summertime and plenty of exciting restaurants. It's also home to a range of vintage shops, art galleries, music venues and McCarren Park on its northern edge.

Blue Bottle Williamsburg

160 Berry Street, Brooklyn, NY 11249 | **Williamsburg**

Photo: Clay McLachlan

One sip of anything here and you'll agree that Blue Bottle's cult following is more than warranted. Blue Bottle has a commitment to taking every step possible to deliver high-quality coffee. This location has a few tables in front of a glass wall, behind which is Blue Bottle's east coast roastery (and bakery). Despite the constant flow of customers, it's a surprisingly relaxed environment. The baristas certainly know what they're doing with milk here, and the cappuccinos are delicious, but the espresso is so flavorful and bright that you've got to try it on its own.

(510) 653-3394
bluebottlecoffee.com
Subway L (Bedford Avenue)

MON–SUN.   7:00am – 7:00pm

First opened 2010
Roaster Blue Bottle Coffee
Machine Custom Slayer
Grinder Mazzer Luigi

Espresso	$3.00
Cappuccino	$4.00
Latte	$4.50

Sister locations Boerum Hill / Bryant Park / Chelsea / Hell's Kitchen / High Line / Met Breuer / Rockefeller Center

MAP REF. 130

139

COFFEE 4.75 / 5   🫘 🫘 🫘 🫘 🫘

OVERALL 4.75 / 5   ★ ★ ★ ★ ★

Charter Coffee

309 Graham Avenue, Brooklyn, NY 11211 | **Williamsburg**

Photo courtesy of the venue

Scott Cameron's background lies in the beverage side of the business, so he's well placed to be running this cozy 20 seater café in the heart of Williamsburg. Raw and reused wood make for a quirky and laid back edge. The espresso is crafted to near perfection and the latte art is fabulous. The bonus: Chrissy Tsang's background is in hair-cutting, and she practices her art on the premises. Sip and clip anyone?

(347) 721-3735
www.chartercoffee.com
Subway L (Graham Ave)

MON–FRI. 7:00am - 7:00pm
SAT–SUN. 8:00am - 7:00pm

First opened 2016
Roaster Counter Culture Coffee
Machine La Marzocco Linea, 2 groups
Grinder Nuova Simonelli Mythos

Espresso $3.00
Cappuccino $3.75
Latte $4.25

MAP REF. **131**

COFFEE 4.25 / 5   🫘🫘🫘🫘🫘 | **OVERALL** 4.25 / 5   ★★★★✬

Devoción

69 Grand Street, Brooklyn, NY 11249 | **Cobble Hill**

TOP
35

Photo courtesy of the venue

You can enjoy the worlds artisan finest Colombian coffees here at this sprawling café, as Devoción sources and purchases all their coffee from Colombia. The shop reflects this focus with its spectacular space, outfitted with its roastery in the front where you can see the roasters hard at work. The main room is an impressive chamber, bursting with sun from a center skylight. The space is huge, with plenty of tables and deliciously sunken-in couches, accented by an incredible living wall, with impressive plants all native to Colombia.

(718) 285-6180
devocion.com
Subway J, Z (Marcy Ave), L (Bedford Ave),
G (Metropolitan Ave)

MON-FRI.	7:00am - 7:00pm
SAT-SUN.	8:00am - 7:00pm

First opened 2014
Roaster Devoción
Machine Kees Van der Westen Mirage,
3 groups
Grinder Ceado E-92

Espresso	$3.25
Cappuccino	$4.25
Latte	$4.75

MAP REF. 132

COFFEE 4.75 / 5		OVERALL 4.75 / 5

Gimme! Coffee Williamsburg

495 Lorimer Street, Brooklyn, NY 11211 | **Williamsburg**

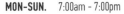

Gimme! Coffee's unassuming design might fool you into thinking that this is just another nice neighborhood coffee joint. In reality it's a decade-and-a-half old branch of an Ithica based roaster that's as serious about the expertise of its baristas as it is the ethics by which they procure their beans. While they meticulously prepare your delicately-flavored pour-over, an amiable barista might tell you about new equipment the farmers purchased with funding provided by Gimme. The maple latte might sound like it's for teenagers, but they use just a touch of syrup, so the sweetness never overpowers the rich flavor of the espresso, insanely delicious.

(718) 388-7771
buy.gimmecoffee.com
Subway L (Lorimer St) or G (Metropolitan Ave)

MON–SUN.   7:00am - 7:00pm

First opened 2003
Roaster Gimme! Coffee
Machine La Marzocco GB5, 3 groups
Grinder Mazzer Luigi

Espresso $3.00
Cappuccino $3.75
Latte $4.00 / $4.50

Sister locations Nolita

MAP REF. 133

COFFEE
4.25 / 5

OVERALL
4.25 / 5

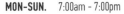

★★★★✦

MatchaBar Williamsburg

93 Wythe Avenue, Brooklyn, NY 11249 | **Williamsburg**

Brothers Wolfgang and Max Fortgang set up in Williamsburg as specialists in matcha tea, but there's a lot more than tea brewing here. Coffee is done properly, espresso and its derivatives only, and the two-group La Marzocco is run with care and skill. The emphasis is on drinks, with just a small selection of sandwiches (weekdays only) and baked goods. Great music from ceiling-level speakers keeps the place humming, with tables at the back the best place to sit, sip, and sound off. Steel rafters complete the picture of industrial-chic, and a bench outside awaits you when the weather's is good.

(718) 599-0015
www.matchabarnyc.com
Subway L (Bedford Ave)

Sister locations Chelsea

| MON–FRI. | 8:00am – 7:00pm |
| SAT–SUN. | 10:00am – 7:00pm |

First opened 2014
Roaster La Colombe Coffee Roasters
Machine La Marzocco Linea, 2 groups
Grinder Mazzer Luigi Major

Espresso	$3.00
Cappuccino	$4.50
Latte	$4.85

MAP REF. **134**

143

COFFEE 4.00 / 5

OVERALL 4.25 / 5 ★★★★☆

Oslo Coffee Roasters Williamsburg

133b Roebling Street, Brooklyn, NY 11211 | **Williamsburg**

Away from the hub of Williamsburg's eat/drink/shop district, but close enough for easy access, this branch of Oslo is a fantastic place to while away the hours. You'll look through big windows fronting the high-ceilinged corner room, with fellow drinkers ranging from solitary workers to lively family groups. The coffee is roasted nearby, from beans bought through direct trade and sold as three house blends. Lovingly brewed into some of New York City's best cups, this Oslo outpost a destination in its own right.

(718) 782-0332
www.oslocoffee.com
Subway L (Bedford Ave)

Sister locations Upper East Side / Williamsburg

| MON-FRI. | 7:00am - 7:00pm |
| SAT-SUN. | 8:00am - 7:00pm (6:00pm in winter) |

First opened 2003
Roaster Oslo Coffee Roasters
Machine Synesso Cyncra, 2 groups
Grinder Mazzer Luigi

Espresso	$3.00
Cappuccino	$3.75
Latte	$3.75

MAP REF. 135

| COFFEE 4.25 / 5 | 🫘🫘🫘🫘◗ | OVERALL 4.50 / 5 | ★★★★✦ |

Parlor Coffee

84 Havemeyer Street, Brooklyn, NY 11205 | **Williamsburg**

Parlor Coffee runs a pop-up shop at this cool Williamsburg barbershop. It's a semi-hidden treasure, as you'll find as you venture beyond the primping and preening. There's a slick but minute espresso bar at the back of the space while keeping up an industrious roastery near the Brooklyn Navy Yard, open for tastings on Sundays. Parlor roast their coffee fresh twice a week, focusing on the natural sweetness and beauty of each batch.

www.parlorcoffee.com
Subway L (Bedford or Lorimer) G (Metropolitan Ave)

Sister locations Brooklyn

| MON-FRI. | 12:00pm - 6:00pm |
| SAT-SUN. | 11:00am - 5:00pm |

First opened 2012
Roaster Parlor Coffee
Machine Kees van der Westen Speedster, 1 group
Grinder Mazzer Luigi Kony

Espresso	$3.25
Cappuccino	$4.25
Latte	$5.00

MAP REF. 136

| COFFEE 4.50 / 5 | 🫘🫘🫘🫘◗ | OVERALL 4.25 / 5 | ★★★★✦ |

Starbucks Reserve Williamsburg

154 North 7th Street, Brooklyn, NY 11211 | **Williamsburg**

For polish and breadth of offering, few places in Williamsburg can match Starbucks. This is their flagship store, one of the locations offering the chain's 'Reserve' range, lots of rare and exquisite single-origin beans. It's also a place where you can think well outside the espresso box, with an exceptionally wide range of alternative brewing methods. You're just as likely to stand in line behind moms pushing strollers as college students on their iPhones. Starbucks may be a global brand, but Starbucks Williamsburg is a genuine local hangout.

www.starbucks.com
Subway L (Bedford Ave)

Sister locations Multiple locations

MON-THU. 5:30am - 9:00pm
FRI-SUN. 5:30am - 10:00pm

First opened 2014
Roaster Starbucks Corporation
Machine Victoria Arduino Black Eagle, 2 groups
Grinder Nuova Simonelli Mythos x2, Ditting

Espresso $3.00
Cappuccino $4.50
Latte $4.50

MAP REF. 137

COFFEE 4.25 / 5		OVERALL 4.50 / 5	

Sweatshop

232 Metropolitan Avenue, Brooklyn, NY 11211 | **Williamsburg**

TOP 35

Williamsburg

Australian-owned Sweatshop is full of things that'll make you smile, from the big neon Sweatshop sign to the 'Death Before Decaf' tote bags, to the hand-painted stool-tops. Smiles continue when you start sipping brews from the sleek La Marzocco espresso machine. The single-origin espresso from Counter Culture Coffee changes every one or two weeks, and latte and macchiato boast exquisite latte art. Food is simple but well executed, with healthy Aussie-style breakfasts giving way at lunch to 'jaffles'(toasted sandwiches). In the words of co-owner Luke, 'We do what we do back home and hope that people dig it.' Full seats both indoors and out suggest they do.

(718) 559-9978
www.sweatshop.nyc
Subway L (Bedford Ave)

MON.	7:00am - 3:00pm
TUE-FRI.	7:00am - 6:00pm
SAT-SUN.	8:00am - 6:00pm

First opened 2014
Roaster Counter Culture Coffee
Machine La Marzocco FB80, 2 groups
Grinder Mazzer Luigi, Mahlkönig EK 43

Espresso	$3.00
Cappuccino	$4.00
Latte	$4.00

MAP REF. 138

COFFEE 4.50 / 5

OVERALL 4.50 / 5 ★★★★⯪

146

Tar Pit

135 Woodpoint Road, Brooklyn, NY 11211 | **Williamsburg**

Photo courtesy of the venue

Tucked away on a residential block in Williamsburg, this best-kept-secret might be the most tranquil, cozy coffee experience in the city. Everything about Tar Pit feels handcrafted - the copper and wood-bric-a-brac-strewn space was designed by the owner, a motorcycle mechanic. The coffee is excellent, from the espresso to the two kinds of cold-brew, to the pour overs (the drip, from Plowshares, is also single-origin). But treat yourself to a cortado - the milk, from Battenkill Creamery, is of such high quality and handled so delicately it's sweeter and smoother than most lattes you'll ever have.

(646) 469-9494
www.tarpitcafe.com
Subway L (Graham Ave)

MON-SUN.   7:00am - 7:00pm

First opened 2011
Roaster Plowshares Coffee Roasters
Machine La Marzocco Linea
Grinder Mazzer Luigi Major

Espresso	$2.50
Cappuccino	$3.75
Latte	$4.00

MAP REF. 139

COFFEE 4.25 / 5	OVERALL 4.25 / 5

Toby's Estate Williamsburg

125 North 6th Street, Brooklyn, NY 11249 | **Williamsburg**

Photo courtesy of the venue

Williamsburg wasn't complete until Toby's came to town. Everything on the menu (both beverage and food) is worth making the trip for, but go for the bright, single-origin espresso, straight up. Trust us, there really is a difference between this and the house blend espresso, especially fresh as the beans are roasted in front of you. Toby's near-flawlessness extends to the friendly, efficient service and the stylish, comfortable, loft-reminiscent design - which is often mobbed with laptops. Before you go, you also have to try the signature flat white, so smooth and rich it takes you to another world.

(347) 457-6160
www.tobysestate.com
Subway L (Bedford Ave)

Sister locations Flatiron / Midtown East / West Village

MON-FRI.	7:00am - 7:00pm
SAT-SUN.	8:00am - 7:00pm

First opened 2012
Roaster Toby's Estate Coffee
Machine Spirit Triplette
Grinder Mahlkönig Guatemala Lab

Espresso	$3.00
Cappuccino	$3.75
Latte	$4.50

MAP REF. 140

COFFEE 4.75 / 5	OVERALL 4.75 / 5
🫘🫘🫘🫘🫘	★★★★✦

148

Upstate Stock

2 Berry Street, Brooklyn, NY 11249 | **Williamsburg**

Almost too-Brooklyn-to-be-true, in the best possible sense, Upstate Stock is a store that sells a selection of home & beauty products, which happens to have a great coffee bar in the front with plenty of seating (a generous touch). This is the only place in America you can get beans from Toronto-based Cut, who tend to roast their beans light, bucking the prevailing trend to dark-roast. The resulting espresso, pulled by a barista who knows what he's doing, is nicely bright. The campfire latte might sound gimmicky but it's essential - touched with delicious smoked maple syrup and sea salt, it truly smells and tastes like summer camp.

www.upstatestock.com
Subway G (Nassau Ave)

MON–SUN. 8:00am – 6:30pm

First opened 2016
Roaster Cut Coffee
Machine Astoria Gloria
Grinder Mazzer Luigi

Espresso $2.50
Cappuccino $3.50
Latte $4.00

MAP REF. 141

COFFEE 4.00 / 5　🫘🫘🫘🫘🫘　**OVERALL** 4.00 / 5　★★★★☆

The Vale Collective

113 North 7th Street, Brooklyn, NY 11211 | **Williamsburg**

The Vale Collective is a clothing store and café rolled into one spacious, high-ceilinged room. You don't have to drink coffee to shop here, but if you do, you'll be well served by the mega-friendly and seriously-expert baristas. There's just one table, a big one, where you can rest your feet after a tour through Williamsburg or settle down with your laptop. But the top attraction, definitely, is the decked garden in the back. This must be one of the best outdoor spaces in Brooklyn; make a beeline there when the weather's good.

(917) 826-3181
Subway L (Bedford Ave)

MON–SUN. 10:00am – 7:00pm

First opened 2015
Roaster Birch Coffee Roasters
Machine La Marzocco FB80, 2 groups
Grinder Mazzer Luigi Super Jolly

Espresso $3.00
Cappuccino $3.75
Latte $3.75

MAP REF. 142

COFFEE 4.25 / 5　🫘🫘🫘🫘🫘　**OVERALL** 4.25 / 5　★★★★☆

Greenpoint & Queens

Growing in popularity, the neighborhoods of Astoria, Long Island City and Greenpoint are hubs of culture, history and lots of good food. Greenpoint adjoins Williamsburg on the other side of McCarren Park and, although quiet, is full of innovative eateries and shops. Walk over Pulaski Bridge to Long Island City and explore a burgeoning part of Queens where lots of new restaurants, MoMA's contemporary art affiliate PS1 and a thriving creative community can be found. Astoria boasts a diverse cultural mix that includes Italian, Jewish and Greek communities.

Greenpoint
Avenue

60 Beans

36-02 Ditmars Boulevard, Queens, NY 11105 | **Astoria**

60 Beans positively bursts with charm. This lovely neighborhood shop takes care of its customers with a real old-school kind of charm and attention. Their beautiful marble-topped bars are equipped with built-in outlets for those diligently working, while their large front windows open fully to let in the breeze when the weather is fine. They use Café Grumpy blends and serve their espressos traditionally, with sparkling water on the side. There's also a beautiful back area with comfy couches and ample sidewalk seating outside too.

(347) 987-3994
www.60beanskitchen.com
Subway N, Q (Astoria - Ditmars Blvd)

MON.	7:00am - 5:00pm
TUE-FRI.	7:00am -10:00pm
SAT-SUN.	8:00am - 11:00pm

First opened 2014
Roaster Café Grumpy Coffee
Machine Kees van der Westen Spirit
Grinder Nuova Simonelli

Espresso	$2.75
Cappuccino	$4.00
Latte	$4.75

MAP REF. 143

| COFFEE 4.25 / 5 | OVERALL 4.50 / 5 ★★★★⯪ |

Astoria Coffee

30-04 30th Street, Queens, NY 11102 | **Astoria**

Astoria Coffee brings a special love for the glorious bean at this neighborhood shop, hosting a variety of different coffees here. They source from multiple American roasters, and have the beans available to purchase. They keep at least two different types of roasts on the bar for espresso drinks. Don't hesitate to ask questions because the baristas are more than happy to walk you through the tasting notes to get you just what you're looking for.

(347) 410-7399
www.astoriacoffeeny.com
Subway N, Q (30th Ave)

| MON-FRI. | 7:00am - 8:00pm |
| SAT-SUN. | 8:00am - 8:00pm |

First opened 2014
Roaster Multi-Roaster
Machine Synesso Hydra
Grinder Mahlkönig EK 43, Mahlkönig K 30

Espresso	$3.00
Cappuccino	$4.00
Latte	$4.00

MAP REF. 144

| COFFEE 4.50 / 5 | OVERALL 4.25 / 5 ★★★★⯪ |

Birch Coffee Long Island City

40-37 23rd Street, Long Island City, NY 11101 | **Long Island City**

You can't actually walk around the beautiful roastery here, but the views, scent, and sounds of it behind glass are exciting enough to bring out every coffee geek's inner child. You can't get beans any fresher than this, and you can taste it in every drink. The espresso is so intense that even the latte has a strong flavor. It's been said that what separates a good barista from a great barista is that a great barista throws out a lot of shots, and on a recent visit, a barista threw out three shots before he felt it was worthy of being served, a testament to Birch's commitment to quality.

(212) 686-1444
www.birchcoffee.com
Subway F (21 St - Queensbridge)

Sister locations Flatiron District / Financial District / Murray Hill / Upper East Side / Upper West Side / West Village

MON-FRI. 8:00am - 5:00pm
SAT-SUN. Closed

First opened 2015
Roaster Birch Coffee Roasters
Machine La Marzocco Linea
Grinder Mahlkönig K 30

Espresso	$3.00 / $4.00
Cappuccino	$3.00 / $4.00
Latte	$3.00 / $4.00

MAP REF. **145**

COFFEE 4.25 / 5	OVERALL 4.25 / 5

Búðin

114 Greenpoint Avenue, Brooklyn, NY 11222 | **Greenpoint**

TOP
35

Photo: Ivor Ip

Búðin is a shop specializing in Nordic coffee, culture, and aesthetic, featuring roasts from Iceland and Norway, as well as home-goods and handmade clothes from Scandinavian purveyors. Coffee beans are all available to buy, should you like to brew some Nordic beans in your own home. The sleek, minimalist space is expansive with plenty of seating and gets beautiful sunlight during the day. In the evenings, Búðin offers a variety of Nordic-related beers too. In the summertime, head out to the backyard for a peaceful paradise.

(347) 844-9639
www.budin-nyc.com
Subway G (Greenpoint Ave)

MON-FRI. 7:00am - 12:00am
SAT-SUN. 8:00am - 12:00am

First opened 2014
Roaster Lofted Coffee, Tim Wendelboe, Koppi, Drop, Good Life, other Nordic Roasters
Machine ModBar
Grinder Mahlkönig EK 43

Espresso $3.00
Cappuccino $4.00
Latte $4.50

MAP REF. 146

COFFEE 4.50 / 5

OVERALL 4.25 / 5 ★★★★⯪

Café Grumpy Greenpoint

193 Meserole Avenue, Brooklyn, NY 11222 | **Greenpoint**

Café Grumpy's original location, in the quiet residential edge of Greenpoint, is so large and the clientele exude such laid-back artsiness that you get the sense you could bring in an easel and start painting a portrait, and no one would raise an eyebrow. Anyone can appreciate the frothy light texture of their latte, but Grumpy, who roast their own beans in the back, cater to coffee nerds. In addition to reliably delicate, rich pour overs (which really do get more flavorful as they cool down), they offer a single-origin espresso in addition to a house blend.

(718) 349-7623
www.cafegrumpy.com
Subway 6 (51st St) or G (Greenpoint Ave)

Sister locations Chelsea / Grand Central Terminal / Lower East Side / Midtown / Park Slope

MON-FRI. 7:00am - 7:30pm
SAT-SUN. 7:30am - 7:30pm

First opened 2005
Roaster Café Grumpy Coffee
Machine Synesso
Grinder Nuova Simonelli Mythos, Mazzer Luigi Robur E

Espresso $3.00
Cappuccino $4.00
Latte $4.50

MAP REF. 147

COFFEE 4.50 / 5	🫘🫘🫘🫘🫘	OVERALL 4.50 / 5	★★★★✦

156

Champion Coffee

142 Nassau Avenue, Brooklyn, NY 11222 | **Greenpoint**

A small but powerful coffee bar at the far end of Greenpoint's Manhattan Avenue, this place makes for a particularly lovely visit when the weather is nice and the garden is open in the back. Champion is a quiet little gem over in this neck of the woods, they use their own blend making it that little bit more special.

(718) 383-3251
www.championcoffee.net
Subway G (Nassau Ave)

MON–SUN. 7:00am – 8:00pm

First opened 2006
Roaster Champion Coffee
Machine La Marzocco, 3 groups
Grinder Mahlkönig

Espresso $3.00
Cappuccino $4.00
Latte $4.50

MAP REF. 148

COFFEE 4.25 / 5 OVERALL 4.25 / 5 ★★★★½

COFFEED Long Island City

37-18 Northern Boulevard, Queens, NY 11101 | **Long Island City**

COFFEED cares about bringing not just great coffee but a sense of community to all its locations. That's why it pairs each café with a local charity and makes an effort to use locally sourced ingredients. Here at the roastery in Long Island City, COFFEED use produce from their rooftop farm as they churn out their fresh roasts constantly throughout the day. They offer four different batch-brewed coffees in house, all fair or direct trade single origins, and in the evenings share refreshing local beers on tap too.

(718) 606-1299
www.coffeednyc.com
Subway E, M, R (36th Street)

Sister locations Multiple New York locations

MON–FRI. 7:00am – 4:00pm
SAT–SUN. 9:00am – 4:00pm

First opened 2012
Roaster COFFEED
Machine La Marzocco Linea
Grinder Mazzer Luigi

Espresso $2.25
Cappuccino $3.50
Latte $3.50

MAP REF. 149

COFFEE 4.00 / 5 OVERALL 4.00 / 5 ★★★★

Gossip Coffee

3704 30th Avenue, Queens, NY 11103 | **Astoria**

With its pristine, 1950's-inspired interior, and beautiful outdoor seating area, Gossip stands out in this neighborhood. Their quality beans are roasted in Queens, just a few miles away. Gossip often offers several types of cold brew, including a "New Orleans style," with vanilla extract and half-and-half, as well as excellent single origin cold brews, which have delicate, fruity, tea-esque flavors. Try them without milk to fully experience their nuance.

(718) 440-8792
www.gossipcoffee.com
Subway N, Q (30th St)

MON-FRI.	7:00am - 9:00pm
SAT-SUN.	8:00am - 9:00pm

First opened 2015
Roaster Gossip Coffee
Machine La Marzocco Strada
Grinder Mazzer Luigi Major

Espresso	$3.00 / $3.50
Cappuccino	$4.00
Latte	$4.50

MAP REF. 150

COFFEE 4.00 / 5	🍩🍩🍩🍩🍩	OVERALL 4.00 / 5	★★★★★

Homecoming

107 Franklin Street, Brooklyn, NY 11222 | **Greenpoint**

Photo courtesy of the venue

Homecoming is a beautiful flower-shop on this busy little stretch of Franklin Street that couples fresh fantastic coffees with their floral arrangements. They serve Sightglass coffee, as well as fine teas, made by charming baristas at this loveable shop. They have a carefully curated selection of home goods here as well, with handmade notebooks, soaps and pots for your plants. It's easy to imagine building your perfect home here, right down to the coffee on the table.

(347) 457-5385
www.home-coming.com
Subway G (Greenpoint Ave)

MON-FRI.	8:00am – 7:00pm
SAT-SUN.	9:00am – 7:00pm

First opened 2013
Roaster Sightglass
Machine La Marzocco Linea, 2 groups
Grinder Mazzer Luigi Robur

Espresso	$3.00
Cappuccino	$4.25
Latte	$4.50

MAP REF. **151**

159

COFFEE 4.00 / 5 🫘 🫘 🫘 🫘 🫘

OVERALL 4.00 / 5 ★★★★☆

Kinship Coffee Cooperative

30-5 Steinway Street, Queens, NY 11103 | **Astoria**

Stumptown Coffee is served at this charming Astoria shop, but they also keep a rotating menu of seasonal single and dual-origins from a variety of roasters. It's got fresh pastries from not one, not two, but three of the very best bakeries in the city, as well as specialty chocolates for good measure. Though the space is small, the shop is bright and has just enough leg room to be a local favorite.

(646) 468-7149
Subway N, Q (30th Ave)

MON-FRI. 7:00am - 9:00pm
SAT-SUN. Closed

First opened 2014
Roaster Stumptown, Heart, Parlor, Sweet Bloom, Supersonic, Tandem, Ceremony
Machine Synesso Cyncra, 2 groups
Grinder Compak K10, Mahlkönig EK 43

Espresso $3.25
Cappuccino $4.00
Latte $4.50

MAP REF. 152

COFFEE 4.50 / 5 🫘🫘🫘🫘🫘

OVERALL 4.25 / 5 ★★★★☆

160

New York City Bagel and Coffee House

40-05 Broadway, Queens, NY 11103 | **Astoria**

You know how some places feel like they've been around forever? Little more than a year old in Astoria, NYC Bagel and Coffee House is one of them. People seem to feel at home here. They come for bagels, sure: outstanding specimens in two sizes (the "mini" is plenty) with loads of interesting fillings. But also for the coffee and baked sweet goods including enticing donuts. Note: though there are no loyalty cards, but "familiar faces get a 'loyalty bonus.'" No wonder 50 per cent of customers are regulars.

(718) 728-9511
www.nycbch.com
Subway M, R (46th St)

Sister locations Astoria

MON–SAT. 6:00am – 10:00pm
SUN. 7:00am – 10:00pm

First opened 2015
Roaster Stone Street
Machine La Marzocco FB80, 3 groups
Grinder Mazzer Luigi Super Jolly

Espresso	$1.75 / $2.25
Cappuccino	$3.25 / $4.00 / $4.50
Latte	$3.25 / $4.00 / $4.50

MAP REF. 153

COFFEE 4.00 / 5

OVERALL 4.25 / 5 ★★★★☆

Propeller

984 Manhattan Avenue, Brooklyn, NY 11222 | **Greenpoint**

Photo: Nicholas Doyle

Propeller is a delightful little café perched on a quiet block in attractive Greenpoint. The decor suggests the darling home of a 1950's flight attendant, accented with commemorative espresso spoons from travels near and far that accompany smart coffees and sweet snacks. The shop hosts working freelancers and artists from around the neighborhood, providing a bright and comfortable environment to work and visit with friends. With a menu of enticing pastries and coffees from local roaster Parlor Coffee, this chic little shop is choice digs for an afternoon boost.

(347) 689-4777
www.cargocollective.com/propellercoffee
Subway G (Greenpoint Ave)

MON-FRI.	7:00am - 4:00pm
SAT-SUN.	8:00am - 5:00pm

First opened 2013
Roaster Parlor Coffee
Machine La Marzocco Linea
Grinder Mazzer Luigi Robur

Espresso	$3.00
Cappuccino	$4.00
Latte	$4.50

MAP REF. 154

COFFEE 4.00 / 5		OVERALL 4.00 / 5

162

The Queens Kickshaw

40-17 Broadway, Queens, NY 11103 | **Astoria**

Photo courtesy of the venue

There's really no reason to ever leave The Queens Kickshaw. This spacious, rough-hewn-wood-filled café starts out in the morning as a coffee bar, serves gourmet grilled cheese, salads and desserts from 10am, and turns into a beer-and-wine bar at night. The baristas really know what they're doing-the espresso drinks are excellent, as are the single-origin pour-overs. It definitely feels like a neighborhood spot, but at the same time is worth going out of your way to experience.

(718) 777-0913
www.thequeenskickshaw.com
Subway E, M, R (Steinway St)

MON-THU.	7:30am - 12:00am
FRI.	7:30am - 1:00am
SAT.	9:00am - 1:00am
SUN.	9:00am - 12:00am

First opened 2011
Roaster Counter Culture Coffee
Machine La Marzocco Strada MP
Grinder La Marzocco Vulcano

Espresso	$3.00
Cappuccino	$4.00
Latte	$4.50

MAP REF. **155**

COFFEE 4.25 / 5   OVERALL 4.25 / 5 ★★★★⯪

Greenpoint & Queens

163

Sweetleaf Greenpoint

159 Freeman Street, Brooklyn, NY 11222 | **Greenpoint**

```
TOP
35
```

Photo: Shawn Breckbill

You can't miss Sweetleaf's recently opened flagship roastery/café, which has the company name stencilled in huge lettering on the exterior. A converted warehouse makes an exceptionally attractive space, wood-beamed and high-ceilinged, and there's plenty of antique seating in both the larger front room and the smaller space in the back, not to mention outside on the benches. Sweetleaf's signature brews are made to a high standard, with lip-smacking cold drinks given equal prominence to the hot stuff. In addition to selling beans, they offer a large range of brewing equipment and coffee making paraphernalia.

(347) 987-3732
www.sweetleafcoffee.com
Subway G (Greenpoint Ave)

MON-FRI.	7:00am - 7:00pm
SAT-SUN.	8:00am - 7:00pm

First opened 2015
Roaster Sweetleaf Coffee
Machine La Marzocco Strada, 2 groups
Grinder Mazzer Luigi Robur E

Espresso	$3.00
Cappuccino	$3.75
Latte	$4.00

Sister locations Williamsburg /
Long Island City

MAP REF.

COFFEE 4.50 / 5		OVERALL 4.75 / 5	

Sweetleaf Center Boulevard

4615 Center Boulevard, Queens, NY 11101 | **Long Island City**

Long Island City is a neighborhood full of very-recently-constructed buildings, but this outpost of Sweetleaf feels like it's been here for decades. At night it turns into a bar serving cocktails and American beers, but during the day it's perfect for parents with babies and freelancers tapping at laptops. True to its name, the espresso at Sweetleaf tastes ever so slightly of honey, and goes down smoothly. Order it straight up or in a macchiato to fully appreciate it.

(347) 527-1038
www.sweetleafcoffee.com
Subway E, M (Court Square, 23rd St)

Sister locations Greenpoint /
Long Island City

MON-THU.	7:00am - 12:00am
FRI.	7:00am - 2:00am
SAT.	8:00am - 2:00am
SUN.	8:00am - 12:00am

First opened 2012
Roaster Sweetleaf Coffee Roasters
Machine La Marzocco GB5, 2 groups
Grinder Mazzer Luigi Robur E

Espresso	$3.00
Cappuccino	$3.75
Latte	$4.00

MAP REF. 157

COFFEE 4.25 / 5   **OVERALL** 4.25 / 5   ★★★★⯪

Sweetleaf Jackson Avenue

10-93 Jackson Avenue, Queens, NY 11101 | **Long Island City**

The prevailing aesthetic in Long Island City is glass and steel, making the cozy design of Sweetleaf all the more welcome. From couches and a table in the front, you can see through big windows into the bakery where excellent cinnamon donuts and other goodies are made. In the back is a room with a record player where guests are encouraged to pick something out from the collection or bring their records to play (no laptops allowed in there). Go for an espresso drink - Sweetleaf roast their own, nearby.

(917) 832-6726
www.sweetleafcoffee.com
Subway G (21st St)

Sister locations Greenpoint /
Long Island City

MON-FRI.	7:00am - 7:00pm
SAT-SUN.	8:00am - 7:00pm

First opened 2008
Roaster Sweetleaf Coffee Roasters
Machine La Marzocco Strada, 2 groups
Grinder Mazzer Luigi Robur E

Espresso	$3.00
Cappuccino	$3.75
Latte	$4.00

MAP REF. 158

COFFEE 4.50 / 5   **OVERALL** 4.50 / 5   ★★★★⯪

Upright Coffee

860 Manhattan Avenue, Brooklyn, NY 11222 | **Greenpoint**

A gem hidden in Greenpoint, Upright balances seriousness with neighborhood amiability. Using their own Upright blend they pour drinks to impress. The space is streamlined and there are only a few stools, hence the shop's name. Though the compact size of the shop might not give you cause to linger, the care and friendliness of the baristas will. Greenpointers are surely lucky to have it.

(718) 215-9910
www.uprightcoffee.com
Subway G (Nassau Ave)

Sister locations West Village

MON-FRI.	7:00am - 7:00pm
SAT.	8:00am - 7:00pm
SUN.	8:00am - 6:00pm

First opened 2011
Roaster Upright Roasting
Machine La Marzocco Linea
Grinder Mazzer Luigi

Espresso	$2.50
Cappuccino	$3.50
Latte	$3.75

MAP REF. 159

COFFEE 4.25 / 5   OVERALL 4.00 / 5 ★★★★☆

Variety Coffee Roasters Greenpoint

145 Driggs Avenue, Brooklyn, NY 11222 | **Greenpoint**

Variety's Greenpoint outlet is almost as small as a café can get, it has seating for just eight. But it's really attractive, with its turquoise wainscoting and bare wood floor, and has a great vibe. The barista describes it as 'intimate and welcoming, but cool,' and that nails it almost perfectly. Milky drinks are expertly handled, but the changing roster of single-origin coffees is a special source of delight.

www.varietycoffeeroasters.com
Subway G (Nassau)

Sister locations Bushwick / Williamsburg

| MON-SUN. | 8:00am - 4:00pm |

First opened 2009
Roaster Variety Coffee Roasters
Machine La Marzocco Linea, 2 groups
Grinder Mazzer Luigi Robur E

Espresso	$2.50
Cappuccino	$3.50
Latte	$4.00

MAP REF. 160

COFFEE 4.50 / 5   OVERALL 4.25 / 5 ★★★★☆

Greenpoint & Queens

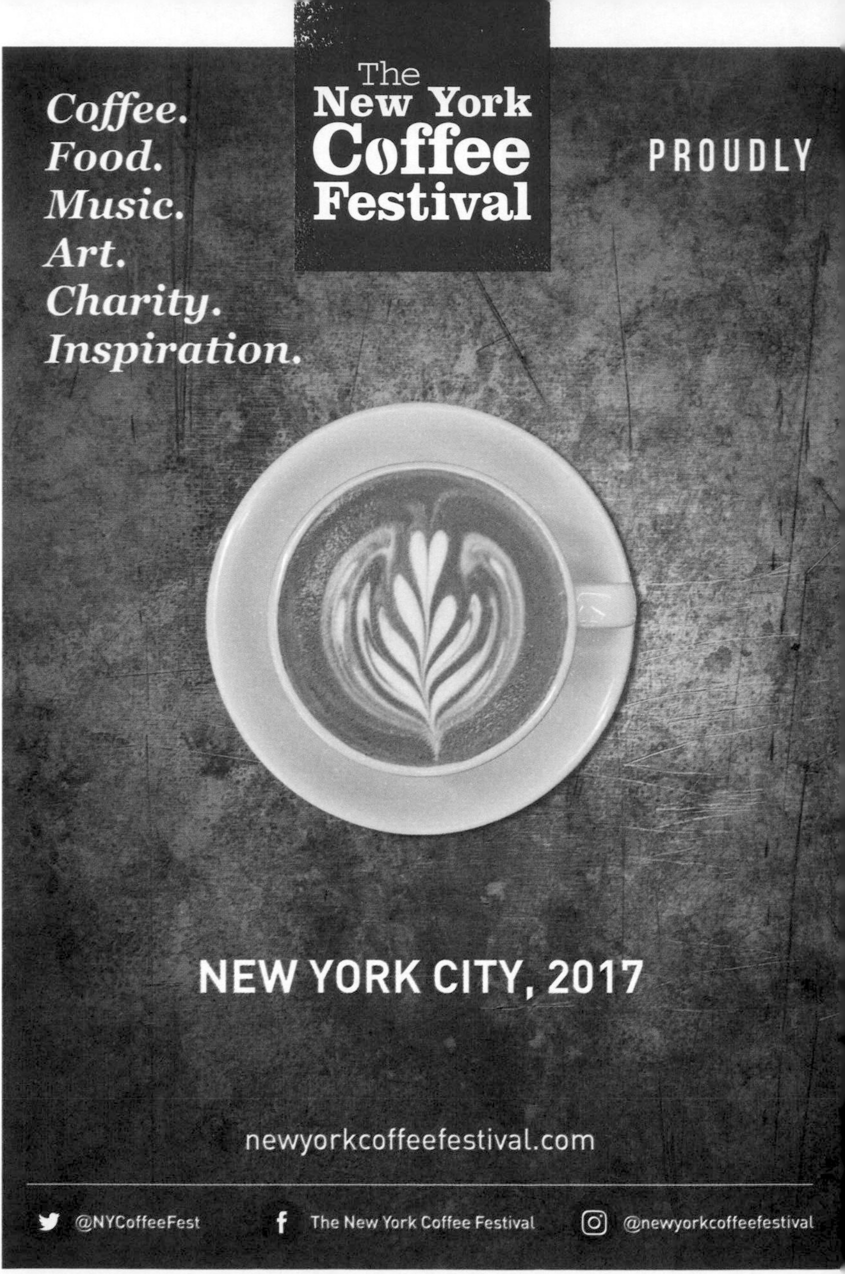
Coffee.
Food.
Music.
Art.
Charity.
Inspiration.
The New York Coffee Festival
PROUDLY
NEW YORK CITY, 2017
newyorkcoffeefestival.com
@NYCoffeeFest
The New York Coffee Festival
@newyorkcoffeefestival

PROJECT
WATER
FALL

BRINGING CLEAN WATER
TO COFFEE GROWING COMMUNITIES

CLEAN DRINKING WATER IS A BASIC HUMAN RIGHT WHICH EVERY PERSON IN THE WORLD SHOULD HAVE ACCESS TO. DESPITE THIS, 663 MILLION PEOPLE CURRENTLY TRY TO SURVIVE WITHOUT IT.

projectwaterfall.org

 @projectwaterf

 Project Waterfall

 @project_waterfall

Coffee Knowledge

Behind every cup of coffee is a unique story. On its journey from coffee tree to cup, coffee passes through the hands of a number of skilled individuals. Over the following pages, expert contributors share their specialist knowledge. As you will see, the coffee we enjoy is the result of a rich and complex process, and there is always something new to learn.

....

Gorilla Coffee

Coffee at Origin

by **Mike Riley**, Falcon Speciality Green Coffee Importers

If you go into New York's vibrant coffee community today and ask any good barista what makes a perfect cup of coffee, they will always tell you that it starts with the bean. Beyond the roasting technique, the perfect grind, and exact temperatures and precision pressure of a modern espresso machine, we must look to the dedicated coffee farmer who toils away in the tropical lands of Africa, Asia and Latin America. They are the first heroes of our trade.

Approximately 25 million people in over 50 countries are involved in producing coffee. The bean, or seed to be exact, is extracted from cherries that most commonly ripen red but sometimes orange or yellow. The cherries are usually hand-picked then processed by various means. Sometimes they are dried in the fruit under tropical sunshine until they resemble raisins - a process known as 'natural'. The 'honey process' involves pulping the fresh cherries to extract the beans which are then sundried, still coated in their sticky mucilage. Alternatively, in the 'washed process', the freshly pulped beans are left to stand in tanks of water for several hours where enzyme activity breaks down the mucilage, before they are sundried on concrete patios or raised beds. Each method has a profound impact on the ultimate flavor of the coffee.

The term 'speciality coffee' is used to differentiate the world's best from the rest. This means it has to be Arabica, the species of coffee that is often bestowed with incredible flavors - unlike its hardy cousin Robusta which is usually reserved for commercial products and many instant blends. But being Arabica alone is by no means enough for a coffee to achieve the speciality tag, since the best beans are usually those grown at higher altitude on rich and fertile soils. As well as country and region of origin, the variety is important too; Bourbon, Typica, Caturra, Catuai, Pacamara and Geisha to name but a few. Just as Shiraz and Chardonnay grapes have their own complex flavors, the same is true of coffee's varieties. Some of the world's most amazing coffees are the result of the farmer's innovative approach to experimentation with growing and production techniques, meaning that today's speciality roaster is able to source coffees of incredible complexity and variation.

A good coffee establishment will showcase coffees when they are at their best - freshly harvested and seasonal, just like good fruit and vegetables. Seasonal espresso blends change throughout the year to reflect this.

As speciality coffee importers we source stand-out coffees by regularly travelling to origin countries. Direct trade with farmers is always our aim. Above all, we pay sustainable prices and encourage them to treat their land, and those who work it, with respect. Such an approach is increasingly demanded by New York's speciality coffee community in order to safeguard the industry's future.

172

Small Batch Roasting

by **Jonathan Withers**, Green Coffee Buyer, Toby's Estate Brooklyn

Coffee roasted in small batches is a pillar of the specialty coffee industry. It's an essential part of how we elevate our product above the classic American perception of coffee as a simple common commodity. At Toby's Estate, we and our customers celebrate a small batch methodology. It is an artisanal, hand-crafted approach that facilitates and advances deep connections between tradesperson and material, removed from the industrial construct of mass production prioritized above quality; fostering instead a relationship with the client centered on a product made-to-order, carefully and skillfully.

Successfully delivering quality with this approach relies on the implementation of systems which are focused towards consistently achieving a high standard - batch to batch and day to day. From the perspective of the customer, quality is only as high as our ability to fulfill every time. Among the artisanal aspects of small batch roasting, experienced craftspeople have the tools at hand to achieve these high degrees of quality; it's only a matter of applying them towards the goal of consistency.

The operation of small batch equipment allows for the manipulation of multiple controls towards the progress and outcome of a roast: heat via gas burners, airflow via fan speed,damper position, drum speed, and chosen batch size. These variables all independently influence the roast and are essential avenues for exploration in obtaining the sweet-spot. That is the reference profile of how to best roast that coffee in production. Too many variables moving at once however, will diminish the roaster's control over the batch. Once this ideal roasting of a coffee is established, reducing the complexity of variables is key. In most production machines, this is commonly achieved by setting all variables other than gas pressure. Then the batch is controlled solely by manipulating the heat applied to the roaster.

Having limited the variables to simplify and improve repeatability, we need points of feedback with which to monitor and react to controls and results during the roast. Temperature readings at multiple points in the roasting system are essential. These are done with a probe that measures the air exiting the drum and a probe placed awash in the beans to measure the temperature of coffee mass. Gauges on the gas supply and roaster exhaust air allow for hard measurements of the values of heat being applied (burners) and removed (airflow). Associating a reference profile to a static batch size allows these values to serve as a meaningful reference. Therefore, we can replicate the precise conditions and adjustments in future production batches. For recording, collating, and parsing all this data, many options exist to digitally log roasting data and display the information as a referable curve. By drawing the current curve over that of the reference, batches can be skillfully manipulated to be precisely replicated.

After the batch is dropped and cooled, other points to control consistency exist to ensure perfect uniformity. Measuring the weight of the roasted coffee against that of the initial green shows the moisture mass lost during roasting. This number will change as the green coffee ages throughout its lifespan, but from day to day it provides a simple metric as to how similarly the coffee was roasted. More precisely, color analyzers exist which optically meter roasted, ground coffee to give a numeric value indicating the degree to which the coffee has roasted. Cupping your roasted product is of course the most direct connection

with the success of the final consistency. Multiple batches appearing together on the same table are incredibly meaningful as they can be directly compared against one another. Carefully recording and collating this sensory data allows a full picture of success as well as areas for focused improvements.

Successfully delivering quality from small batch roasting relies on the skills, talent, and experience of the operator. Yet to ensure that this artistry is maintained and guaranteed with every batch over long days and weeks, a rigorous system of variable control, monitoring metrics and tight quality control is paramount. When they catch problems, you're glad the mistakes weren't able to slip through the cracks.

Coffee Grinding

by **Jeremy Challender**, Co-owner and Director of Training, Prufrock Coffee and the

Grinder technology is about to change radically. Machine design, techniques behind the bar and hand brewing methodology have improved rapidly over recent years. Manufacturers are starting to address this by seeking feedback from users as well as lab testing. Home users can benefit from these changes too. New designs entering the market have drawn directly from the experiences of barista champions. Grinder designers are seeking professional and consumer feedback on taste, flavor and ergonomics through direct collaboration and field testing. Manufacturers are aware that we need development to continue and, now more than ever, baristas have a voice in this process. To be a barista in this time of grinder development is very exciting.

With all brew methods the challenge is replicating flavor and strength. Once we've got a precise brew recipe for a coffee we stand a better chance of extracting our coffee consistently. Commercially, the easiest way to navigate from this baseline towards the optimum extraction level is with micro-adjustments in the exposed surface area of the grinds - so the grinder is key to managing flavor in the cup.

The challenge grinder designers face is how to create consistency of grind size and shape. If you get out the microscope, and a set of test sieves, you start to realize all your grinds aren't the same size, nor are they all the same shape. If they were all the same size and shape, brewing would be much easier to control. In espresso you will have seen tiny granules in your cup that are smaller than the holes in the filter basket. We call these fines. These small particles have very high surface area and extract very quickly. As a home brewer, you could consider following the example of many championship baristas; invest in laboratory test sieves to remove a portion of particles under a certain size to reduce over-extracted flavors.

There is a portion of particles that fit side-on between the burrs and are planed rather than ground. We call these larger particles boulders. They have a much lower surface area relative to their size and in a 30 second espresso extraction will under-extract. Wobbly hand grinders are real offenders in the production of boulders. These too can be sieved out.

Sharp burrs are considered to reduce fines production. Ceramic burrs, which many hand grinders are fitted with, are very durable but are often not very sharp to start with. The material of choice at the moment is titanium-coated steel. Large burr diameter is linked to lower production of fines and boulders (more 'modal' distribution) so enormous bag grinders are being examined for application in espresso making. Cutting systems like spice grinders produce a very high proportion of fines and boulders, so are not recommended.

Keeping the coffee cool during grinding is a challenge. Burrs get hot in use because of friction, and some of the most exciting developments recently have focused on temperature stability of the burrs and burr casing with the addition of heating elements and fans. A warm grinder behaves differently to a cold or a hot one, so the particle shape and size are dependent on both grind setting and temperature.

Modern grinder design is very focused on ease of access for regular cleaning. Arabica coffee has up to 17% fat content. We only extract a small percentage of this into a beverage but even after a day of commercial use, a grinder will have a slick of fats and tiny fine particles built up around the burr casing and the barrel and throat of the grinder. Oils oxidise, so grinders must be opened up and thoroughly swept out on a regular basis. Burrs can be washed in soapy water or coffee cleaner, or abrasive oil absorbing grinder cleaning granules can be used. Home baristas have an advantage here by being able to clean after a few shots rather than after a full day's usage.

The final hurdle to overcome is grind retention: many grinders on the market have large barrels and throats that can store as much as 40g of grinds that must be squeezed out before fresh grinds appear. At Prufrock, we are moving away from grinders with a high retention of grinds as we are looking to optimize freshness. When grind changes are required we want the benefit of micro-adjustment to be immediate. Here, home baristas are also well placed, as hand grinders have zero retention of grinds and some very high quality espresso hand grinders are now available on the market.

Over the last decade we have felt that machine technology has been in advance of grinders. We often comment that a barista's top priority should be the choice of grinder. Find a great grinding solution and great coffee will follow.

Photo: Jacob Thue

176

Water - The Enigma

by **Maxwell Colonna-Dashwood**, Co-owner, Colonna and Small's, UK Barista Champion 2012 & 2014

This vital ingredient is the foundation of every cup of coffee you have ever tasted, apart from the bean itself of course.

It's not just coffee that relies so dramatically on this everyday and seemingly straightforward substance. The worlds of craft beer and whiskey are suitable comparisons, with breweries and distilleries proudly signifying the provenance of their water as being a vital part of their product.

A roaster, though, sells coffee, the water bit comes post sale. The water will be different and unique based on the locality of brewing, and this is on top of all of the other variables that define coffee brewing such as grinding, temperature and brew ratios. The reality is that the impact of water is rarely directly witnessed, with the other variables often being seen as the cause for dramatic flavor changes. You may be wondering right now, how big an impact can it really have?

I'm yet to present the same coffee brewed with different waters to drinkers and not have them exclaim "I can't believe how different they are, they taste like different coffees'. These aren't "coffee people" either, but customers who contested prior to the tasting that "you may be able to taste the difference but I doubt I can tell."

It may make you question whether the coffee that you tried and weren't particularly keen on, was a representative version of what the bean actually tastes like, or at the least what it is capable of tasting of like.

So, why the big difference, what is in the water?

Nearly all water that trickles out of a tap or sits in a bottle is not just water. As well as the H2O there are other bits and bobs in the water. Minerals mainly. These have a big impact not only on what we extract from the coffee but also how that flavor sits in the cup of coffee.

It's fair to say that currently the way the coffee industry discusses water is through the use of a measurement called Total Dissolved Solids (TDS).

TDS has become the measurement which is relied upon to distinguish and inform us about how water will affect our coffee. It gives us a total of everything in the water. The problem though, is that TDS doesn't tell us everything we need to know about the water; it doesn't tell us about what those solids are. On top of this, TDS meters don't measure some non-solids that have a huge impact on flavor.

In the water, we need the minerals calcium and magnesium to help pull out a lot of the desirable flavor in the coffee, but we also need the right amount of buffering ability in the water to balance the acids. This buffering ability can be noted as the

bicarbonate content of the water.
So for example an "empty" soft water with no minerals will lack flavor complexity and the lack of buffer will mean a more vinegary acidity.

However the coffee shops in this guide will most likely have a trick up their sleeve. The industry filtration systems that have been developed primarily to stop scale build up in the striking and valuable espresso machines, also produce water compositions that are more often than not preferable for coffee brewing. Speciality coffee shops require all manner of specifics to be obsessed over and carefully executed. That cup of coffee that hits you and stops you in your step with intense, balanced and complex flavor will owe its

brilliance to careful brewing, a knowledgeable brewer and superb equipment. However, it also owes a significant part of its beautiful character and flavor to the water it is brewed with.

Brewing Coffee at Home

by **Christian Baker, David Robson, Sam Mason & The New York Coffee Guide**

....

You may be surprised to know that coffee brewed at home can rival that of your favorite coffee shop. All you need is good quality ingredients and some inexpensive equipment. Keep in mind that small variations in grind coarseness, coffee/water ratio and brew time will make a significant difference to flavor, and that trial and error is the key to unlocking perfection.

Whole Beans: Whole bean coffee is superior to pre-ground. Coffee rapidly deteriorates once ground, so buy your coffee in whole bean form and store it in an air-tight container at room temperature. It should be consumed between three and thirty days after roast and ground only moments before brewing.

Water: Water is important because it makes up over 98% of the finished drink. Only use bottled water, preferably with a dry residue between 80-150mg/l. It will inhibit your ability to extract flavor and reveal only a fraction of a coffee's potential.

Digital scales: Get a set of scales accurate to 1g and large enough to hold your coffee brewer. Coffee is commonly measured in 'scoops' or 'tablespoons', but coffee and water are best measured by weight for greater accuracy and to ensure repeatability. Small changes in the ratio of coffee to water can have a significant impact on flavor. A good starting point is 60-70g of coffee per litre of water. Apply this ratio to meet the size of your brewer.

....

Grinder

A burr grinder is essential. Burr grinders are superior to blade grinders because they allow the grind coarseness to be set and produce a more consistent size of coffee fragment (critical for an even extraction). As a general rule, the coarser the grind the longer the brew time required, and vice versa. For example, an espresso needs a very fine grind whereas a French Press works with a coarser grind.

French Press

Preheat the French Press with hot water, and discard. Add 34g of coarsely ground coffee and pour in 500g of water just below boiling point (201-203°F). Steep for 4 to 5 minutes then gently plunge to the bottom. Decant the coffee straight away to avoid over-brewing (known as over-extraction).

AeroPress

The AeroPress is wonderfully versatile. It can be used with finely ground coffee and a short steep time, or with a coarser grind and a longer steep time. The latter is our preferred method for its flavor and repeatability. Preheat the AeroPress using hot water, and discard. Rinse the paper filter before securing, and place the AeroPress over a sturdy cup or jug. Add 16g of coffee and pour in 240g of water at 203°F. Secure the plunger on top, creating a seal. Steep for 3 minutes then plunge over 20 seconds.

Pour Over

We recommend using a pouring kettle for better pouring control. Place a filter paper in the cone and rinse through with hot water. Add 15g of coffee and slowly pour 30g of 203°F water to pre-soak the coffee grounds. This creates the 'bloom'. After 30 seconds add 250g of water, pouring steadily in a circular motion over the center. It should take 1 minute and 45 seconds to pour and between 30-45 seconds to drain through. The key is to keep the flow of water steady. If the water drains too quickly/slowly, adjust the coarseness of the grind to compensate.

Stovetop

A stovetop will not make an espresso, it will, however, make a strong coffee. Pour hot water in to the base to the fill-line or just below the pressure release valve. Fill the basket with ground coffee of medium coarseness (between Pour Over and French Press). Traditional wisdom suggests a fine grind in pursuit of espresso, but stovetops extract differently to espresso machines and grinding fine is a recipe for bitter, over-extracted coffee. Screw the base to the top and place on the heat. When you hear bubbling, remove immediately and decant to ensure the brewing has stopped.

Illustrations: Zoë Barker

Traditional Pump Espresso Machine

Traditional pump espresso machines are ideal for that barista experience to create espresso-based coffee at home. Coffee should be freshly and finely ground and dosed into single or double shot filter baskets. It is then tamped to extract full flavor aroma and coffee crema. The machine controls temperature for a more consistent cup. To enjoy milk drinks such as flat whites and cappuccinos simply froth fresh milk using the steam wand (stay below 158°F) and top up your espresso.

Bean to Cup Machine

Bean to Cup provides the perfect 'coffee shop' fix and fast. It gives you all the versatility of choice and personalization of a traditional pump machine. At the touch of a button, it burr-grinds fresh beans and froths milk (some machines even have a built in carafe), creating a fresh taste for your cup. You can personalize the strength, length, temperature, and even the froth setting. One-touch drink options make your personalized coffee time and again, without mess or fuss.

Latte Art

by **Jai Lott**, Coffee Director for Bluestone Lane

L atte art is the barista's signature in a milk based espresso drink.

Over the years latte art has shifted from being 'etched' chocolate sauce designs and foamy 'hand spooned' structures, to a fragile and carefully constructed pattern where the slightest movement of the hand can make or break a masterpiece.

There are 3 major components to world-class latte art: espresso, milk and execution.

1 Espresso

Perfect espresso is your canvas. Well-executed fresh extraction with a thick stable crema sets the foundation for your latte art. A double shot or around 40 grams of yield and medium roast is a great starting point. This helps create contrast in the cup. Espresso and milk preparation should happen simultaneously to ensure crema does not have time to dissipate.

2 Milk

The colder your milk, the better. This gives it more chances at rotation in the pitcher before reaching temperature, which in turn increases your milk's texture. Once the steam wand is in position slightly below the surface of the milk and sits slightly off center, engage the wand and slowly lower the jug adding small amounts of air while simultaneously keeping the milk spinning solid. All air should be added prior to the milk reaching room temperature for great results. Turn off the steam when you reach your desired temperature.

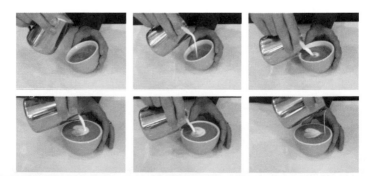

Ideal learning tools:

- A steaming pitcher that has perfect spout symmetry. Using the same jug every time is vital to getting comfortable with latte art.

- A wide ceramic cup of around 8oz is great to start with. This gives you plenty of breathing space.

- An environment where you can concentrate and not be bumped!

3 Execution

If everything worked out (and trust me it takes practice even getting to this point) you should have beautiful espresso and a hot pitcher with milk resembling freshly applied paint. Its time to pour!

Tilting the cup at 45 degrees, pour into the center of the espresso at a height of 2-3 inches. Imagine a diving board and a diver trying to pierce the espresso without disrupting the surface. Keep an even flow for the entire pour.

Once the cup gets to the low edge of the cup, two things need to happen:

Firstly, flatten out the cup while simultaneously bringing the pitcher all the way down to almost full contact with the espresso. This will increase the amount of microfoam allowed from behind the pitchers spout and a white dot will begin to appear (remember keep the same flow the whole time!)

Secondly, in the final moment of the pour, exit the cup by lifting the jug and cutting through the center of your white dot. Imagine the milk from the spout is an airplane taking off.

Perfect love heart!

Once you master our love hearts, move on to a two-stack tulip.

The big secret - stick to one design for days, weeks if needed. Get each design mastered before progressing to the next. This is the way to get good fast and an understanding of what each movement will result in.

Spill milk, make a mess and most importantly have fun! That's what coffee should be all about. Just don't forget that latte art certainly makes coffee look great, but great espresso and milk are more important!

What Does 'Local' Coffee Mean?

by **Teresa von Fuchs**, Sales Director at Volcafe Specialty

When the Eastman Egg Company in Chicago revamped their coffee program, they didn't partner with a company from Chicago. Even though there are great roasters in the area, they found that the partnership that met all of their goals and matched their values was New York. This got them thinking about ways to quickly explain this choice to their customers and what 'local' means in coffee.

Local coffee isn't as straightforward as local eggs, local arugula or even local bread (which may or may not contain locally grown and milled grain!). By necessity, coffee must travel hundreds and thousands of miles. Most people who drink coffee every day in the U.S. have never seen a coffee tree in person – they might not even know that coffee starts as a fruit. Given the distance from the source, it's challenging for most people to truly grasp the vast amount of work that must happen before coffee ends up in your cup. Yet it's this connection and understanding to where something comes from and how it's made that people seek when they look for 'local' products.

In the journal "Renewable Agriculture and Food Systems" CJ Peters writes, "Most researchers accept that eating locally means minimizing the distance between production and consumption." When the Food Marketing Institute conducted a study asking Americans across the country why they buy local; knowing where a product came from was in the top three responses. Supporting the local economy came in second. While it's logistically not possible to actually shorten the distance between where coffee is grown and all the places it's consumed, there are ways to bring producers and consumers closer together. For coffee, 'local' is about relationships and knowledge, not 'locale.'

For the team at Eastman, it was the connection their new roasting partner helped forge with the farms and people growing and processing their coffee that helped them answer the questions about why their roaster wasn't 'local.' It wasn't about where the roastery was located. It was about developing a connection to the process from seed to cup that made their coffee more local.

What I love about this lens is that it can extend everyone's experience of coffee, not just café owners looking for a roaster. When you go to your local café, the staff know you. They remember what you drink, your name, what days or times you usually come in, snippets of conversations you've shared. It's your café. And that café is your opportunity for local coffee. Whether your want to know the exact altitude of the farm where the coffee was grown or not, you can still participate in minimizing the distance between the production of coffee and drinking it. Get to know your barista. What do they drink? Why do they work there? What do they like about coffee?

If you buy beans from a store to brew at home, find out about the roaster. Where do they get the beans from? How did they start roasting coffee? What do they love about it?

The longer I work in coffee, the more expanded my idea of "local" and "community" becomes. When I taste coffee, I think about the places and the people that grow the coffee, all the hands that pick and process and pack and ship that coffee. I think about how far it travels to where it will be roasted. I think about who roasted it. When I go to a café for coffee, I think about all that, as well as the care and time someone took to craft it into a cup. When I sip, I feel connected to that whole world.

Espresso

by **Bill McAllister**, Director of the Service Department, Irving Farm Coffee Roasters

··

The definition of espresso is a method of brewing coffee according to the Specialty Coffee Association of America, a trade group that represents and undoubtedly has some direct connection to every person and place in this book. Yet the difference between a coffee made using a Chemex versus a vacuum pot or any other coffee maker is negligible compared to what an espresso machine produces. The root cause is pressure. Espresso machines take water that would normally be poured or sprinkled onto coffee and forces it through the pressure of the atmosphere. But who came up with that? How did they know it could make coffee so much more delicious than normal?

The etymology of espresso reveals a lot about the intention of this technology. If we Anglicize the word into "expresso", it is easy to see that the drink needs to be made quickly, but also that it needs to be made expressly for a consumer. Back in Italian, it's just as easily interpreted as "to press out", bringing pressure back into the picture. Put it all together, and you have a device that makes coffee quickly, one at a time, using pressure. All of this is according to Andrea Illy (yes, that Illy) as written in Espresso Coffee, one of the few textbooks on coffee.

It paints a somewhat primitive picture of Italy in the 1880s, where the first patents for espresso machines are traced. The technology at the time was coarse and rugged. It relied on huge boilers heated by fire that used a head of steam to push water through the ground coffee. A barista would be hard-pressed to make anything that wasn't quite bitter. This was espresso for decades. But then, manufacturers introduced a lever and piston as an alternative method of generating pressure. This change allowed the machines to be much smaller, brew at pressures that have become today's standard, and use water that isn't super-heated. All of a sudden espresso carts became a reality, bringing the means of caffeination to even more people. But the most important part of the change in the machines is that it is no longer impossible for a shot to be pulled that is more than something used as a dose of energy.

The espresso of today and its potential to be mind-blowingly delicious has a culture surrounding it that elevates it above the rest of coffee. Cafes have moved far beyond just dishing out shots to give workers a boost mid-afternoon. A coffee shop that wants to be the talk of the town these days draws customers in by talking about the specific farms their coffee is from, the agronomy of the plant from which the coffee is harvested, and a level of precision that requires scales that wouldn't be out of place in a display on St Marks Place.

How we went from pre-industrial caffeine machines relying on levers and pistons to today's models doesn't contain any big eureka moments, but is mostly a steady stream of smart revisions. Baristas realized early on that their ability to reliably make the most delicious espresso they've tasted required having a machine they could count on to work the same way every time. To this end, springs and levers were replaced by electric pumps and gas burners were replaced by heating elements controlled by computers. Yet with all of these, advances were driven by the trial and error of passionate baristas, because despite the long history of espresso, there is not a lot of scientific writing about the process with which it is made. When a handful of videos featuring clear plastic portafilters started trickling out in the last few years, coffee pros everywhere were astounded - the first real evidence in over a century as to what's happening when making espresso!

Explanations of how and why espresso works may be lacking, but we can still gather a few lessons as consumers. A properly prepared shot looks elegant as it pours into a cup, flowing thick but steady, like warm honey, a promise of flavor that delivers on the intoxicating smell characteristic of coffee shops everywhere. At its best, a coffee brewed as espresso sees its flavors held under a magnifying glass. The experience is intense, but often divisive: fruity Ethiopian coffees taste like someone plopped jam in the bottom of your demitasse, so lush with fruit flavor and sweetness it seems impossible that the only ingredient is coffee. The second you sip a good espresso, all thoughts of history are fleeting memories; you thoughts are now on the delicious beverage in your hands.

Coffee History in New York City

by **Erin Meister**, Coffee Professional, Journalist & Author of a forthcoming book about NYC's coffee

What makes New York a coffee town, exactly? Is it the reputation as the "city that never sleeps," or the fact that caffeine is necessary to get anything done in a New York minute? Do residents of the city drink an estimated 25 percent more coffee than anyone else in the country because the stuff can be bought on every street corner? Or could it be the other way around - that the sheer ubiquity of the stuff is what makes it practically a way of life for locals? Does it mean something that the average cup costs less than a copy of the daily paper?

No matter the reason, facts are facts: New York and coffee are made for each other.

Of course it's true that the regular Joes here simply love their "regular" joe (which usually means a cup of drip with milk and sugar, in deli shorthand). But there's actually more coffee flowing in the veins of the city than even gets poured on its surface. So much of what happens with coffee here is behind-the-scenes that most New Yorkers don't even know quite how caffeinated they really are. Even the history of the city and the beverage go all the way back - further, actually, than the name "New York." The coffee habit actually got brewed up when the city was still New Amsterdam, under Dutch control.

From the green-coffee contracts to the containers they come in, to the roasting machines that turn them from hard little seeds into semi-precious brown beans, New York has had a tremendous influence on every step in the journey of billions of bags, brews, and cups.

The city's position as an East Coast hub has allowed for its unique junction of caffeine and culture, not only just among its fellow American metro centers, but also worldwide. The coffee history here has influenced global market structures, supply and demand trends, shipping routes and intercontinental trade, roasting and preparation technology and innovation, marketing strategy, and even cafe life. The first truly successful commercial coffee-roasting machine was patented by a New Yorker, Jabez Burns, whose company would go on to become one of the most enduring and consistently innovative in the industry for over 130 years. The Green Coffee Association of New York was founded as the first significant overseeing body to ensure, and insure, the integrity and fulfillment of contracts. Depending on whom you ask, the first espresso machine in the country was imported and installed either uptown at Barbetta Restaurant in 1911 or downtown at Caffè Reggio, which opened in 1927.

The combination of a crush of people from all types and all walks, overwhelming sparking creative energy, and the fearlessness of failure is certainly in part to thank, but coffee itself contributes something to the dynamic and living nature of New York - it keeps the gears turning.

There is also a special something about New York City that not just allows for rebirth and reinvention, but actually thrives on it. Perhaps the most classic "only in New York" moments in the timeline of coffee's history here is the fact that one of the very men who was responsible for the first tremendous "coffee collapse" in 1880 – a failed attempted corner on the coffee market by a syndicate of large brokerage houses, the result of which was widespread bankruptcy and at least one alleged coffee suicide – was elected just two years later to serve as the first president of the Coffee Exchange, which his misadventure had inspired the coffee men to create.

That's only one of hundreds of "only in New York" stories, of course. Here's another in 1907, a woman named Alice Foote MacDougall used her last $38 to establish herself as the only female coffee broker in the waterfront Coffee District. Within two decades she was signing a $1 million lease on her fifth hugely successful coffee shop – the modern equivalent of nearly $14 million. Just like the city itself, MacDougall was a beautiful mess of contradictions. Though she was a successful business owner herself, she regularly advised women to stay at home and out of the commercial and corporate worlds, and was an ardent anti-suffragist.

From coffeehouse counter-culture in the late 1950s and 1960s, to the Central Perk-inspired, overstuffed, mismatched café of the 90s, to the minimal and coffee-quality-obsessed espresso and slow-pour bars of the early 2000s; NYC coffee shops have always managed to define their era. They have been capturing and capitalizing on the shifting moods and cravings of 8 million people, even if only for a finite period. The coffee lovers of today in Brooklyn, Manhattan, and Queens (the Bronx and Staten Island will catch up eventually) go about their daily rituals, drinking their morning cups or evening espresso, knowing full well that there's no telling what will be on the next generation of menus, in the next wave of shops.

Beyond the bars, there are the beans. Millions and millions of bags of them that travel through New York every year, on their way to roasters and consumers around the country and world. Despite the fact that New Jersey actually claims the country's first fully containerized shipping port, this transformed the intercontinental transit of loads of green coffee and knocked a few pegs out of NYC's dominance in that arena.

Even the world's most famous mermaid has a Brooklyn connection: Starbucks chairman and CEO Howard Schultz grew up in the Canarsie section of the borough – a neighborhood that perhaps ironically remains a good-coffee desert today, but even that will surely change with time.

Gotham's inexhaustible need to create, destroy, and re-create might make it difficult to keep up with the trends (or "waves," if we must). But at least we can all be assured that the revolutions will be caffeinated. "There is something in the New York air that makes sleep useless," wrote Simone de Beauvoir in 1947, and it's as true today as it was then, only the answer is obvious. It must simply be the coffee.

Coffee Glossary

Acidity: the pleasant tartness of a coffee. Examples of acidity descriptors include lively and flat. One of the principal attributes evaluated by professional tasters when determining the quality of a coffee.

AeroPress: a hand-powered coffee brewer marketed by Aerobie Inc., and launched in 2005. Consists of two cylinders, one sliding within the other, somewhat resembling a large syringe. Water is forced through ground coffee held in place by a paper filter, creating a concentrated filter brew.

Affogato: one or more scoops of vanilla ice cream topped with a shot of espresso, served as a dessert.

Americano, Caffè Americano: a long coffee consisting of espresso with hot water added on top. Originates from the style of coffee favored by American GIs stationed in Europe during WWII.

Arabica, Coffea arabica: the earliest cultivated species of coffee tree and the most widely grown, Arabica accounts for approximately 70% of the world's coffee. Superior in quality to Robusta, it is more delicate and is generally grown at higher altitudes.

Aroma: the fragrance produced by brewed coffee. Examples of aroma descriptors include earthy, spicy and floral. One of the principal attributes evaluated by professional tasters when determining the quality of a coffee.

Barista: a professional person skilled in making coffee, particularly one working at an espresso bar.

Blend: a combination of coffees from different countries or regions. Mixed together, they achieve a balanced flavor profile no single coffee can offer alone.

Body: describes the heaviness, thickness or relative weight of coffee on the tongue. One of the principal attributes evaluated by professional tasters when determining the quality of a coffee.

Bottomless portafilter, naked portafilter: a portafilter without spouts, allowing espresso to flow directly from the bottom of the filter basket into the cup. Allows the extraction to be monitored visually.

Brew group: the assembly protruding from the front of an espresso machine consisting of the grouphead, portafilter and basket. The brew group must be heated to a sufficient temperature to produce a good espresso.

Brew pressure: pressure of 9 bar is required for espresso extraction.

Brew temperature: the water temperature at the point of contact with coffee. Optimum brew temperature varies by extraction method. Espresso brew temperature is typically 194-203˚F. A stable brew temperature is crucial for good espresso.

Brew time, extraction time: the contact time between water and coffee. Espresso brew time is typically 25-30 seconds. Brew times are dictated by a variety of factors including the grind coarseness and degree of roast.

Burr set: an integral part of a coffee grinder. Consists of a pair of rotating steel discs between which coffee beans are ground. Burrs are either flat or conical in shape.

Café con leche: a traditional Spanish coffee consisting of espresso topped with scalded milk.

Caffeine: an odorless, slightly bitter

alkaloid responsible for the stimulating effect of coffee.

Cappuccino: a classic Italian coffee comprising espresso, steamed milk and topped with a layer of foam. Traditionally served in a 6oz cup and sometimes topped with powdered chocolate or cinnamon.

Capsule: a self-contained, pre-ground, pre-pressed portion of coffee, individually sealed inside a plastic capsule. Capsule brewing systems are commonly found in domestic coffee machines. Often compatible only with certain equipment brands.

Chemex: A type of pour over coffee brewer with a distinctive hourglass-shaped vessel. Invented in 1941, the Chemex has become regarded as a design classic and is on permanent display at the Museum of Modern Art in New York City.

Cherry: the fruit of the coffee plant. Each cherry contains two coffee seeds (beans).

Cold brew: Cold brew refers to the process of steeping coffee grounds in room temperature or cold water for an extended period. Cold brew coffee is not to be confused with iced coffee.

Cortado: a traditional short Spanish coffee consisting of espresso cut with a small quantity of steamed milk. Similar to an Italian piccolo.

Crema: the dense caramel-colored layer that forms on the surface of an espresso. Consists of emulsified oils created by the dispersion of gases in liquid at high pressure. The presence of crema is commonly equated with a good espresso.

Cupping: a method by which professional tasters perform sensory evaluation of coffee. Hot water is poured over ground coffee and left to extract. The taster first samples the aroma, then tastes the coffee by slurping it from a spoon.

Decaffeinated: coffee with approximately 97% or more of its naturally occurring caffeine removed is classified as decaffeinated.

Dispersion screen, shower screen: a component of the grouphead that ensures even distribution of brewing water over the coffee bed in the filter basket.

Dosage: the mass of ground coffee used for a given brewing method. Espresso dosage is typically 7 10g of ground coffee (14-20g for a double).

Double espresso, doppio: typically 30-50ml extracted from 14-20g of ground coffee. The majority of coffee venues in this guide serve double shots as standard.

Drip method: a brewing method that allows brew water to seep through a bed of ground coffee by gravity, not pressure.

Espresso: the short, strong shot of coffee that forms the basis for many other coffee beverages. Made by forcing hot water at high pressure through a compressed bed of finely ground coffee.

Espresso machine: in a typical configuration, a pump delivers hot water from a boiler to the brew group, where it is forced under pressure through ground coffee held in the portafilter. A separate boiler delivers steam for milk steaming.

Extraction: the process of infusing coffee with hot water to release flavor, accomplished either by allowing ground coffee to sit in hot water for a period of time or by forcing hot water through ground coffee under pressure.

Coffee Glossary contd.

Filter method: any brewing method in which water filters through a bed of ground coffee. Most commonly used to describe drip method brewers that use a paper filter to separate grounds from brewed coffee.

Flat white: an espresso-based beverage first made popular in Australia and New Zealand. Made with a double shot of espresso with finely steamed milk and a thin layer of microfoam. Typically served as a 5-6oz drink with latte art.

Flavor: the way a coffee tastes. Flavor descriptors include nutty and earthy. One of the principal attributes evaluated by professional tasters when determining the quality of a coffee.

French press, plunger pot, cafetiere: a brewing method that separates grounds from brewed coffee by pressing them to the bottom of the brewing receptacle with a mesh filter attached to a plunger.

Froth, foam: created when milk is heated and aerated, usually with hot steam from an espresso machine's steam wand. Used to create a traditional cappuccino.

Green coffee, green beans: unroasted coffee. The dried seeds from the coffee cherry.

Grind: the degree of coarseness to which coffee beans are ground. A crucial factor in determining the nature of a coffee brew. Grind coarseness should be varied in accordance with the brewing method. Methods involving longer brew times call for a coarse grind. A fine grind is required for brew methods with a short extraction time such as espresso.

Grinder: a vital piece of equipment for making coffee. Coffee beans must be ground evenly for a good extraction. Most commonly motorised, but occasionally manual. Burr grinders are the best choice for an even grind.

Group: see Brew Group

Grouphead: a component of the brew group containing the locking connector for the portafilter and the dispersion screen.

Honey process, pulped natural, semi-washed: a method of processing coffee where the cherry is removed (pulped), but the beans are sun-dried with mucilage intact. Typically results in a sweet flavor profile with a balanced acidity.

Latte, caffè latte: an Italian beverage made with espresso combined with steamed milk, traditionally topped with foamed milk and served in a glass. Typically at least 8oz in volume, usually larger.

Latte art: the pattern or design created by pouring steamed milk on top of espresso. Only finely steamed milk is suitable for creating latte art. Popular patterns include the rosetta and heart.

Lever espresso machine: lever machines use manual force to drive a piston that generates the pressure required for espresso extraction. Common in the first half of the 20th century, but now largely superseded by electric pump-driven machines. Lever machines retain a small but passionate group of proponents.

Long black: a coffee beverage made by adding an espresso on top of hot water. Similar to an Americano, but usually shorter and the crema is preserved.

Macchiato: a coffee beverage consisting of espresso 'stained' with a dash of steamed milk (espresso macchiato) or a tall glass of steamed milk 'stained' with espresso (latte macchiato).

Macrofoam: stiff foam containing large bubbles used to make a traditional cappuccino. Achieved by incorporating a greater quantity of air during the milk steaming process.

Matcha: Finely ground powder of specially grown and processed green tea. The matcha plants are shade-grown for three weeks before harvest.

Microfoam: the preferred texture of finely-steamed milk for espresso-based coffee drinks. Essential for pouring latte art. Achieved by incorporating a lesser quantity of air during the milk steaming process.

Micro-lot coffee: coffee originating from a small, discrete area within a farm, typically benefiting from conditions favorable to the development of a particular set of characteristics. Micro-lot coffees tend to fetch higher prices due to their unique nature.

Mocha, caffè mocha: similar to a caffè latte, but with added chocolate syrup or powder.

Natural process: a simple method of processing coffee where whole cherries (with the bean inside) are dried on raised beds under the sun. Typically results in a lower acidity coffee with a heavier body and exotic flavors.

Over extracted: describes coffee with a bitter or burnt taste, resulting from ground coffee exposed to hot water for too long.

Peaberry: a small, round coffee bean formed when only one seed, rather than the usual two, develops in a coffee cherry. Peaberry beans produce a different flavor profile,

typically lighter-bodied with higher acidy.

Piccolo: a short Italian coffee beverage made with espresso topped with an equal quantity of steamed milk. Traditionally served in a glass.

Pod: a self-contained, pre-ground, pre-pressed puck of coffee, individually wrapped inside a perforated paper filter. Mostly found in domestic espresso machines. Often compatible only with certain equipment brands.

Pour over: a type of drip filter method in which a thin, steady stream of water is poured slowly over a bed of ground coffee contained within a filter cone.

Pouring kettle: a kettle with a narrow swan-neck spout specifically designed to deliver a steady, thin stream of water.

Portafilter: consists of a handle (usually plastic) attached to a metal cradle that holds the filter basket. Inserted into the group head and locked in place in preparation for making an espresso. Usually features a single or double spout on the underside to direct the flow of coffee into a cup.

Portafilter basket: a flat bottomed, bowl-shaped metal insert that sits in the portafilter and holds a bed of ground coffee. The basket has an array of tiny holes in the base allowing extracted coffee to seep through and pour into a cup.

Puck: immediately after an espresso extraction, the bed of spent coffee grounds forms compressed waste matter resembling a small hockey puck.

Pull: the act of pouring an espresso. The term originates from the first half of the 20th century when manual machines were the norm, and baristas pulled a lever to

Coffee Glossary contd.

create an espresso.

Ristretto: a shorter 'restricted' shot of espresso. Made using the same dose and brew time as for a regular espresso, but with less water. The result is a richer and more intense beverage.

Roast: the process by which green coffee is heated in order to produce coffee beans ready for consumption. Caramelization occurs as intense heat converts starches in the bean to simple sugars, imbuing the bean with flavor and transforming its color to a golden brown.

Robusta, Coffea canephora: the second most widely cultivated coffee species after arabica, robusta accounts for approximately 30% of the world's coffee. Robusta is hardier and grown at lower altitudes than arabica. It has a much higher caffeine content than arabica, and a less refined flavor. Commonly used in instant coffee blends.

Shot: a single unit of brewed espresso.

Single origin, single estate: coffee from one particular region or farm.

Siphon brewer, vacuum brewer: an unusual brewing method that relies on the action of a vacuum to draw hot water through coffee from one glass chamber to another. The resulting brew is remarkably clean.

Small batch: refers to roasting beans in small quantities, typically between 4-24kg, but sometimes larger.

Speciality coffee: a premium quality coffee scoring 80 points or above (from a total of 100) in the SCAA grading scale.

Steam wand: the protruding pipe found on an espresso machine that supplies hot steam used to froth and steam milk.

Stovetop, moka pot: a brewing method that makes strong coffee (but not espresso). Placed directly on a heat source, hot water is forced by steam pressure from the lower chamber to the upper chamber, passing through a bed of coffee.

Tamp: the process of distributing and pressing ground coffee into a compact bed within the portafilter basket in preparation for brewing espresso. The degree of pressure applied during tamping is a key variable in espresso extraction. Too light and the brew water will percolate rapidly (tending to under extract), too firm and the water flow will be impeded (tending to over extract).

Tamper: the small pestle-like tool used to distribute and compact ground coffee in the filter basket.

Third wave coffee: the movement that treats coffee as an artisanal foodstuff rather than a commodity product. Quality coffee reflects its terroir, in a similar manner to wine.

Under extracted: describes coffee that has not been exposed to brew water for long enough. The resulting brew is often sour and thin-bodied.

V60: a popular type of pour over coffee brewer marketed by Hario. The product takes its name from the 60° angle of the V-shaped cone. Typically used to brew one or two cups only.

Washed process: one of the most common methods of processing coffee cherries. Involves fermentation in tanks of water to remove mucilage. Typically results in a clean and bright flavor profile with higher acidity.

Whole bean: coffee that has been roasted but not ground.

A-Z List of Coffee Venues

A-Z List of Coffee Venues contd.

A-Z List of Coffee Venues contd.

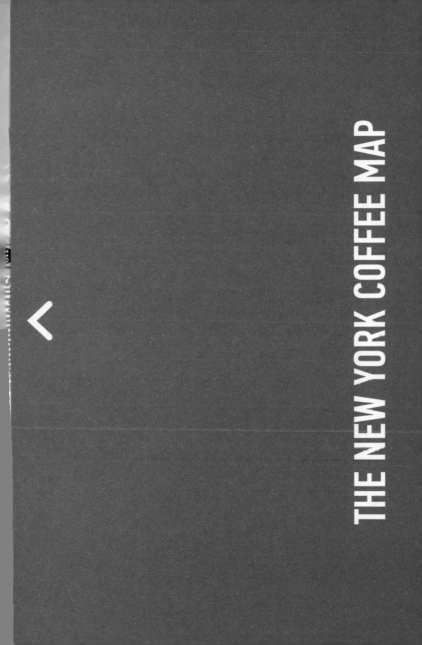

THE NEW YORK COFFEE MAP

Notes, sketches, phone numbers etc.